10th Anniversary Edition

HOW TO BE
BRILLIANT

Change your ways in 90 days!

MICHAEL HEPPELL

PEARSON

Harlow, England • Lond͏   ͏ ͏ ͏ ͏ ͏ ͏ ͏ ͏ ͏ San Francisco • Toronto • Sydney
Auckland • Singapo͏   New Delhi
Cape Tow͏   Paris • Milan

PEARSON EDUCATION LIMITED

Edinburgh Gate
Harlow CM20 2JE
United Kingdom
Tel: +44 (0)1279 623623
Website: www.pearson.com/uk

First published in Great Britain 2004 (print)
Second edition published 2007 (print)
Third edition published 2011 (print and electronic)
Fourth edition published 2014 (print and electronic)

© Pearson Education Limited 2004, 2007 (print)
© Michael Heppell 2011, 2014 (print and electronic)

The right of Michael Heppell to be identified as author of this work has been asserted by him in accordance with the Copyright, Designs and Patents Act 1988.

Pearson Education is not responsible for the content of third-party internet.

ISBN: 978-1-292-06520-5 (print)
       978-1-292-06521-2 (PDF)
       978-1-292-06522-9 (ePub)
       978-1-292-06523-6 (eText)

British Library Cataloguing in Publication Data
A catalogue record for this book is available from the British Library

Library of Congress Cataloging-in-Publication Data
Heppell, Michael.
  How to be brilliant : change your ways in 90 days! / Michael Heppell. -- 4 Edition.
  pages cm
  Includes index.
  ISBN 978-1-292-06520-5 (pbk.) -- ISBN 978-1-292-06522-9 (ePub) -- ISBN 978-1-292-06523-6 (eText)
  1. Success. 2. Success in business. 3. Self-actualization (Psychology) I. Title.
  BF637.S8H43324 2014
  158--dc23
                                        2014024450

The print publication is protected by copyright. Prior to any prohibited reproduction, storage in a retrieval system, distribution or transmission in any form or by any means, electronic, mechanical, recording or otherwise, permission should be obtained from the publisher or, where applicable, a licence permitting restricted copying in the United Kingdom should be obtained from the Copyright Licensing Agency Ltd, Saffron House, 6–10 Kirby Street, London EC1N 8TS.

The ePublication is protected by copyright and must not be copied, reproduced, transferred, distributed, leased, licensed or publicly performed or used in any way except as specifically permitted in writing by the publishers, as allowed under the terms and conditions under which it was purchased, or as strictly permitted by applicable copyright law. Any unauthorised distribution or use of this text may be a direct infringement of the author's and the publishers' rights and those responsible may be liable in law accordingly.

10 9 8 7 6 5 4 3 2 1
18 17 16 15 14

Text design by Design Deluxe
Cover design by Jem Butcher
Cartoons by Steve Burke

Typeset in Helvetica LT Std 9/12pt by 3
Printed in Great Britain by Henry Ling Ltd, at the Dorset Press, Dorchester, Dorset

NOTE THAT ANY PAGE CROSS REFERENCES REFER TO THE PRINT EDITION

For finding brilliance in everything,

I dedicate this book to the love of my life, Christine,

and to our children, Michael and Sarah

CONTENTS

About the author vi

So why a Tenth Anniversary Edition? vii

Introduction xi

1 A brilliant life balance 1
2 The five characteristics of brilliant people 13
3 Brilliant goal-setting 39
4 Time to be brilliant 49
5 Brilliant belief systems 63
6 Brilliant rock-busting 71
7 I need your help 81
8 Brilliant values 91
9 Brilliant teams 103
10 Brilliant vision 111
11 Brilliance into action: Time for a review 123
12 How to be 'brilliant-er': The next level! 127
13 Overcoming obstacles: What stops brilliance? 135
14 Brilliant life lessons 141
15 Brilliance uncovered 151

How to Be Brilliant exercise checklist 158
Appendix: Michael Heppell Ltd company values 160
Thank you to … 162
Index 165

ABOUT THE AUTHOR

Described as the cure for an average life and as one of the top three professional speakers in the world, **MICHAEL HEPPELL** is taking people development to a new level.

He is the international bestselling author of seven books: *How to Save an Hour Every Day*, *Flip It*, *How to Be Brilliant*, *Five Star Service*, *How to Have a Brilliant Life* and *The Edge – how the best get better* and *Future Proof Your College*.

His clients and advocates include FTSE 100 companies, business leaders, top athletes, TV personalities and film makers. His website **www.michaelheppell.com** and associated tools are used by thousands of people every day who want to improve their quality of life. His mission is to positively influence 1,000,000 lives.

As a professional speaker he wows his audiences with his humour and industry savvy. His style was described at the London Business Forum as 'like shot-gunning a bucket of espresso' and from Melbourne to Manchester, he guarantees to have audiences off their seats and taking action.

He lives in Northumberland, England, with his wife and business partner Christine.

SO WHY A TENTH ANNIVERSARY EDITION?

When I wrote *How to Be Brilliant* I would have been thrilled if anyone other than my Mum had bought it. Now *How to Be Brilliant* has been a bestseller for a decade and I have been stunned at the results. It has been translated into over 20 different languages, it's available in bookshops in more than 80 countries around the world and has had multiple reprints. So why change a winning formula?

As you'll read, part of the ethos of *How to Be Brilliant* is to keep on moving to the next level, and I thought this book could be even better. The first major change is the focus. The original book was written for a business audience and spent several years as a top-10 selling business book. But business wasn't the main reason why people were reading it. People want to know how to be brilliant in *all* areas of their life, so now we've refined the book to work as a guide to help you to be brilliant whoever you are, and whatever you are doing.

I've given the manuscript a facelift, chopped out some of the good bits (that will make sense to you later) and questioned some of the ideas and their relevance today.

To really understand what is different it's probably a good idea to go back 10 years and discover how it all began.

How it all began

I lied; not a big lie you understand, but it was still an untruth. But if I hadn't lied then the chances are you wouldn't be reading this book now.

Let's go back a few years.

It was early spring 2003 and I'd just met with a mentor of epic proportions. His name is Sir David Bell and at that time he was Director of People at

Pearson plc. (I'll tell you more about mentors as you read *How to Be Brilliant*.) Sir David was keen to help me. In fact, he was so keen he set up an introduction with Pearson's top Publishing Editor, Rachael Stock.

Move on a couple of weeks and picture the scene:

I'm in the Malmaison Hotel, Leeds, and Rachael and I are enjoying lunch. I'm telling her all about my amazing idea for a book – it's called 'How to Be Brilliant'!

She's excited, I'm excited, the staff in 'Mal' are excited – but there's a challenge. Pearson are one of the biggest publishers in the world and Rachael is very busy. She tells me it could be a year before my book would make it into their packed publishing schedule.

This wasn't part of my plan. I'd set a goal that by 2004 I would be a published author (there's a whole chapter on setting goals in this book) and, like the Mountie always getting his man, I always achieve my goals.

Then Rachael gave me a glimmer of hope. A moment of opportunity arose so I pounced, and that's when I told my untruth.

Over coffee, Rachael said she loved the idea of 'How to Be Brilliant' and what a shame the manuscript wasn't ready because another author had failed to meet their writing deadline and she had been left with one publishing 'slot'.

'Oh, it is ready', I fibbed.

'It's strange you didn't mention that', Rachael said, 'I thought you were just planning the book.'

'Sorry Rachael, I should have said it's done. And If I could grab that publishing slot, could we go for it and get it published this year?'

It was Maundy Thursday, and an hour after I'd left Leeds I found myself on the A1, stuck in traffic and thinking about what I'd committed to.

What terrified me most wasn't the fact that in a moment of madness I'd committed to having a 50,000-word manuscript of a book that wasn't written to my new publisher by the following Tuesday. It was having to explain to my wife that we'd need to cancel everything because that weekend we were doing something 'new and exciting'. We were writing a book!

And here's why I'm the luckiest man in the world. Within 10 minutes of making the announcement, my wife (Christine) had cleared the decks, arranged activities for the kids and established a plan that would see us writing 18 hours a day for the entire Easter weekend.

The plan was simple. I would brain dump everything I knew about 'How to Be Brilliant' and she would turn it into something a reader could actually understand and enjoy.

We roped in help from everywhere we could and set to work (see Chapter 7 about the best way to ask for help). Believe me we used those 'magic words' a dozen times that weekend.

Ten years (and 7 books) later, we still use the same writing method (although our last book took four years to write rather than four days). One of the chapters you'll read in *How to Be Brilliant* is called 'Brilliant teams'; over that Easter weekend we were the embodiment of a brilliant team.

We printed and posted the manuscript to Rachael and she, too, took massive action and completed the first edit in just two days. You can imagine my excitement when the 'red pen' editor's version arrived back just a week after we'd agreed the deal.

Then my heart sank.

Imagine an A4 file filled with 150 pages of your 'finest' work. Now imagine every page covered in red pen. Modified, amended and revised as if an over-zealous English professor had been asked to mark a primary school pupil's recollection of 'What I did this summer'.

In hindsight she was right about everything she wrote. She pointed out exactly what needed to be: chopped, changed, shortened, lengthened, explained more clearly, backed up with evidence, etc.

My favourite comment was what she wrote about Chapter 4. I remembered working on Chapter 4; it was two in the morning and I said to Christine, 'I think this chapter needs a bit more – I'll pad it out'. So I did – by around 1000 words. Which is probably why Rachael wrote, *'There's a problem with the beginning and end of this chapter ... they're too far apart. Can you lose about 1000 words please?'*

How wonderful.

The irony is I was writing a book called 'How to Be Brilliant', not how to be quite good, not too bad or plain indifferent. And, as you'll see in the coming pages, being brilliant often means your current best is just not good enough.

Not a day goes by that we don't receive a note, comment or email from someone who has read the book and wants to share what it has meant to them. It's truly humbling.

So, 10 years on what's changed?

'Everything' would be the easy answer. Ten years ago if I'd asked you to 'Tweet' about *How to Be Brilliant* or 'Like my page on Facebook', you would have thought I'd gone mad. In the last 10 years we've experienced a global economic crisis, seen household names cease trading and witnessed the World Wide Web become a global platform for anyone with something to say.

Yet most of the subjects I write about in *How to Be Brilliant* remain exactly the same. In fact, some of the chapters in this edition have barely been touched – they didn't need a facelift. A few others were ready for their 10-year make-over and I've updated these using all the insights I've gleaned over the years from what works and what doesn't.

I've added a '**Ten Years On**' box to the end of each chapter. I wanted to share how my thoughts and ideas have developed and how my life has changed since Christine and I first wrote the manuscript over that busy Easter weekend.

I've met many interesting people during this time and had the opportunity to share and have my ideas challenged at hundreds of live events. I've questioned my core beliefs – they remain the same, but I've added more depth to the core principles I first wrote about 10 years ago.

My main belief remains the same: good is no longer good enough. If you really want to make a difference and get the very best out of every opportunity, then you have to be brilliant.

So what will Rachael Stock think reading this, 10 years on? Well, the truth is Rachael and I became great friends and one day I plucked up the courage to tell her about my 'of course I've finished the manuscript' fib. She gave me a knowing look and said, 'Do you really think I didn't know? Come on Michael, you'd just spent an hour telling me how brilliant people get out of their comfort zones, use pace, smash through limiting beliefs and take massive action. As much as I knew you hadn't yet written it, I believed that you could and was certain you would.'

MICHAEL HEPPELL

INTRODUCTION

Fed up with life being distinctly average? Is good not good enough any more? Do you want more than just feeling that you're 'getting by'?

Then you're in the right place. If you're putting in an lot of effort for measly rewards or feel that life and work are a struggle with little to show for it then I have some good news for you. And if you're feeling a distinct lack of happiness or success then you need to know the secret of brilliance.

Looking at people achieving remarkable things – those getting recognition, reward and success, or people who have such a positive influence on everyone around them – it's easy to think they are just lucky. The truth is far from that. Their secret is that they decided to be brilliant. And you can do the same.

How to Be Brilliant will give you the tools to find out exactly where you are now. Then you'll work out where it is you want to get to and develop strategies and powerful methods to get you there:

★ as quickly as possible

★ as economically as possible

★ with as much fun as possible.

You'll change your ways in 90 days

You'll discover the specific characteristics of brilliant people so that you can learn and model from the best. Through many examples and personal stories, you'll discover how to use techniques to overcome the barriers that hold you back. You'll learn how to set a clear plan for an outstanding, brilliant future, and how to communicate with your friends, colleagues and family at a higher level.

With this foundation you'll create a vision and have an exciting 90-day plan to achieve your short-term goals. Then with a range of tried and tested tools and with new levels of energy and enthusiasm, you can move forward to create and achieve longer-term goals. You'll learn how to be proactive when faced with challenges and have over 50 tools at your disposal to move you to the level where you deserve to be.

Also in this special edition you'll learn how those who are already brilliant work hard to be even better. Brilliance is a standard, not a skill. You'll be able to take the techniques learned for one area of your life and apply the same standards in other areas with minor adjustments – easy, once you know the secrets to being brilliant.

The book is designed to be easy to use and is broken down into sections ensuring you learn at your own pace. 'Brill Bits' are designed to pull out key pieces of insight, learning or things you may want to look at more closely. So make a commitment now, and enjoy reading *How to Be Brilliant*.

Getting the most from this book

This book can really change your life. But to do so, you need to participate fully. If I suggest to you that you should do something specific, then please just do it. Just sitting there reading this information isn't going to be enough. One of the things I know about my own personal life is that understanding something on an intellectual level is worthless.

This book is full of exercises, check points and prompts for you to take some time out to reflect. Make sure you take a moment or two to complete these important parts of the *How to Be Brilliant* process.

Life is about taking actions. It's about doing something – anything! That's what's going to make the difference. It's the actions that you take now that are going to affect your life massively in the future. Just acknowledging information is not enough.

The secret's not in the knowing, it's in the doing.

BRILL BIT

Let me tell you what we're going to cover in this book.

First of all I want you to look at getting a brilliant life balance. You'll do an exercise called the Wheel of Life. The Wheel of Life isn't something that you're only going to do once. In fact, this whole programme isn't something you're only going to do once. This is something that I would like you to do on a regular basis. Every time you visit your Wheel of Life you'll understand how your own personal development is improving. If you spot areas that you're starting to fall back on a little, you can immediately address those issues and fix them.

You're going to explore the characteristics of brilliant people. What is it that makes a person brilliant? Do you think they are born brilliant? Or do you think they have characteristics that they put in place, certain things that they learn, and certain things that they strive for that make them brilliant? There are five key characteristics of brilliant people. If you apply those characteristics to your life, you are certain to move up to the next level. I'll guarantee you will move closer towards brilliance.

Then you'll do some goal-setting. You need a strong 'Why?' to move forward and engage in the tools and techniques. Clear goals are the best drivers.

You won't learn a system for goal-setting that is like the majority of others, because in my experience the majority of goal-setting systems don't work. You'll not see any SMART* goals here!

Then you're going to look at the level at which you currently live your life. Are you doing a poor job? Are you doing a good job? Are you doing a fantastic job? Or are you doing a brilliant job? The people who are doing a consistently brilliant job get the best results by far. In this book you'll discover how to get brilliant results every time.

One of the things that stops you from getting brilliant results right now is probably your belief system. It's not for me to say whether your belief system is right or wrong. However, I know through experience, working with thousands and thousands of people, that it's your belief system that holds you back more than anything else. You created that belief system. In *How to Be Brilliant* you're going to explore what it is that you believe and most importantly why you believe it.

Wouldn't it be great if you could change your belief system right now and make it more empowering; a belief system designed by you, exclusively for you, that helps you engage your life at an altogether different level? You'll explore this later in the book.

You're going to study Circles of Influence versus Circles of Concern. We all have many concerns in our lives, but the way to move on is to look at what you can influence, what you can change and the actions you can take rather than dwelling on your concerns and things you can't alter. You are going to put together a strategy, using a model that will move you forward very quickly. In fact, at a pace that will surprise you. When you read this book again as a reminder in a month, two months, or a year's time, you'll look back and think, 'Wow, look how much I've changed!' The reason why you will have changed, and changed for the positive, is that you'll have worked on areas that you can personally influence in your life.

Moving through the book, you're going to explore your values system. Values are something that you create. You create values in the same way

---

*SMART goals, meaning Specific, Measurable, Achievable, Realistic, with a Timescale, have been taught by trainers, usually corporate, for years now. They are great for outcome setting when you are running a project, but I have yet to meet a person who is currently living their life's vision through using only the SMART system.

you create a belief system, and then you find the evidence and the rules that support a belief system and that support your value system. So you're going to look in depth at your values, and understand how you created them in the first place.

You'll understand how the decisions you make every moment of every day make you the person you are. You'll make decisions about your current values that may change your life for ever. You might be lucky. You could read the 'Brilliant values' chapter and say, 'That's me, right now, perfect values, perfect rules, I'm perfect!' Or maybe you'll be like 95 per cent of the population and say, 'Hold on a moment, they're not the right values, they're not the values that are going to get me to where I really need to be in my life.' You'll need brilliant values if you want to be brilliant in life.

And why do this on your own? The 'Brilliant teams' chapter will give you a range of techniques to help you work with others, get people on your side and save time. Blended with some cracking ideas for building rapport with others, this chapter is a must for anyone who deals with other human beings. That's all of us then!

Then I will encourage you to step up and set some big goals – stretch goals that at first may seem impossible – but with the application of the ideas contained on these pages, you'll soon see outstanding results.

You'll discover how to use an amazing visualization technique called mental rehearsal: the same method used by top performers. Brilliance doesn't happen by accident: it happens for a reason. Mental rehearsal will show you how you can create the outcomes that you want on a consistent basis. It is based on the techniques and systems of the very best people on the planet; the people who really know how to get results in an exciting and passionate way. I want to show you how you can set goals that really excite you, encourage you to take action and get the results that you desire.

Towards the end of the book, you put your brilliance into action and create enough personal leverage to make things happen.

In this revised edition you can read a selection of success stories from people who, just like you, made a decision to read this book. Plus there's some detailed instruction on how to get people to help you and a chapter on brilliant life lessons.

True will and false will

When you make any decision you will do so with either true will or false will. Let me explain the difference. False will is the most common. It's when people say they definitely will do something. Easy to say … True will means you will do it no matter what happens. I once had an incredible coach and mentor called Peter Field. For the first year Peter seemed to focus entirely on how to build my 'true will' muscle. This meant that every time I said I would do something, deep down inside, I knew I had to do it. Come what may.

It works. Once this metaphoric muscle is strong it becomes much easier to take on new commitments, to know that you will see things through, and your confidence soars. The challenge is you, like me, probably find it easier to exercise the false will muscle. As a result you don't see things through, you procrastinate and in the end you blame outside forces such as time, lack of resources or other people for where you are.

My challenge to you is to use *How to Be Brilliant* to build your true will muscle. Really commit to whatever you say you'll do. Use the ideas in this book to give you confidence, belief in yourself and – most importantly – a new benchmark to live your life.

Finally, I want to negotiate a little contract with you before we start properly.

Take a moment and give yourself a very honest mark out of 10 for how happy you are to learn new information: 10 is high, 0 is low.

★ If you have a passion for education, you go out of your way to gain new knowledge and you're a lifelong learner, then well done you – that's a ·high mark.

★ Or it could be that you are happy to learn new things if you need them. That's a mid-way mark.

★ Or you could be reading this and thinking, 'I'm sure my brain is full! I can't get any more in there.' That would be a low mark ...

Then give yourself a mark out of 10 for how happy you are to change. How do you feel about change?

★ Is change something that you absolutely relish, that you love? Are you happy to try any new idea? When they say 'There's going to be a change programme', at work, if you're the one shouting, 'Yes, I love that' then give yourself a high mark.

★ Or you may be thinking 'I'm happy to change, but only the things that are wrong. If it ain't broke don't try to fix it.' That's OK – give yourself a mid-way mark.

★ If you're not as happy about change, or if you don't want to change the way that you do things, give yourself a low mark.

Then take those two numbers and multiply them together. You'll have a number somewhere between 0 and 100.

If you have 100 at this point, congratulations, there's no doubt that you'll get maximum value out of this book. If you are a 90, great, once again you can expect wonderful results. Between 80 and 90, you're doing well. Now as

BRILL BIT

Understanding the ideas in the book is fine. Your ability to put those ideas into action is what makes the big difference. So test yourself and go for it!

we start to get lower, I bet the area that lets you down is your willingness to change. That's not true in all cases; however, most people dislike change.

90 days of massive action

Let me introduce you to the concept of a 90-day massive action plan. The 90-day plan contains the actions you *must* take, not that you *should* take. In 90 days you can make huge shifts in your life and make a significant difference to your circumstances. Check today's date. Count forward 90 days and mentally mark the completion of your first 90 days.

Ninety days is a great timeframe as it's long enough to change any personal habit, most circumstances and every belief. But it's short enough to remain excited. It's like a campaign for a better life. You truly can change your ways in 90 days. You'll hear a lot about 90 days in this book.

Finally, please, please, please, please – I'm on my knees with hands clasped here – do not think this is a one-off exercise. If I were to suggest that all you have to do to be fit is to go to the gym once, would you believe me? Wouldn't that be wonderful? Dream on! If you want to get physically fit and stay fit, you

BRILL BIT

This is a programme for life. Just like being physically fit, being mentally fit requires constant work. But it's worth it!

have to exercise on a regular basis. It's exactly the same with exercising your own personal development. You must work continuously. Every day, every week, every month, making sure you are immersing yourself with information and practising what you learn.

With this in mind – take action now. Decide it's time to change. Make a commitment right here, right now, to play full out. Make a commitment right here, right now, to improve your life, to step up to the next level and learn how to be brilliant.

A BRILLIANT
LIFE BALANCE

Let's begin with one of the simplest but most effective ideas in personal development – the Wheel of Life. This is a way you can measure your own personal development in eight key areas.

You start by working out where you are now in each area; this helps you identify where your efforts need to be directed. And by reviewing how you score on a regular basis, you'll be able to see the progress you're making as it happens, and you'll be sure you're on the right track.

On the opposite page you'll see a blank Wheel of Life. You're going to give yourself a mark out of 10 on each one of the spokes when I describe what each one means. You have to be honest. It's going to be a mark somewhere between 0 and 10. A 0 means it can't get any worse and will be right in the centre of the wheel. A 10 is perfect – life doesn't get any better in this area – and 10s are on the edge of the wheel. The more honest you are with this process, the more you can chart your own personal growth. Later, after you have completed your first wheel, you can take some time to imagine how you would like your wheel to look in the future – this will help massively when we get into the goal setting chapters later in the book.

> **BRILL BIT**
>
> This is PERSONAL development. The more honest you are with yourself, the better the results. To move forward effectively you have to recognize honestly where you are right now.

Now take your Wheel of Life (you can download additional copies at **www.michaelheppell.com**), read the description of each section in turn and then give yourself a mark out of 10.

Health

Are you the type of person who wakes up easily in the morning and shouts, 'Yes. It's a Monday and I've got so much energy'? You then leap out of bed, dive down the stairs, get your kit on and run two or three miles to get the day started. On your return you have a nice shower. You're feeling great, and when you see yourself in a mirror, you just can't help thinking, 'I'm looking good.' You get in to work or you go to school and people are saying to you 'Wow! I just don't believe how well you look.' You are just so vibrant. Everybody else around you could be dropping like flies with the flu. But not you, you're the one with the amazing immune system – you're always well. If that is truly you, if you're that type of person who really plays full out, gets to the end of the day and still has loads of energy, congratulations, you are a 10!

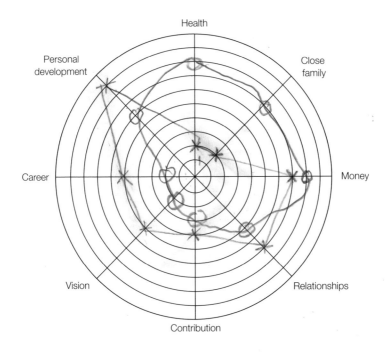

Health

Personal development

Close family

Career

Money

Vision

Relationships

Contribution

But wait, perhaps you are the type of person who is woken from a restless night's sleep by the intrusive alarm clock. As soon as you hear the 'beep beep beep …' the first thing you do is hit the snooze button for nine more minutes of slumber bliss. It starts again, 'beep beep beep …'. You hit snooze again, another nine minutes, heaven. But nine minutes later the damn thing goes off again, 'beep beep beep'. This time you think, 'If I get ready really really quickly, maybe skip breakfast, then I can have nine more minutes!' It's a plan, so you click snooze one more time. It only feels like seconds then it goes off again. This time your irrational, exhausted mind is thinking, 'If I don't have a shower …' You eventually get out of bed to get ready.

As you walk past the mirror, you have a quick look and think, 'Oh my goodness, when did that happen?' You drag yourself to work (or school, college, etc.). You feel a little bit of a sniffle coming on. Immediately you know what that means: 'It's that flu bug that's going round. I'm going to be ill tomorrow.'

For the rest of the day you just drag yourself through. You get home, absolutely trashed. Your 'balanced meal' takes three minutes on high power and your biggest decision of the night is: red or white? Eventually you crash down on the sofa where your idea of relaxation equals watching mindless TV.

If that's you, the bad news is you are probably around a 2 or a 3. The good news is you're not a 1 – those people are too sick to even read! Nevertheless, give yourself a very honest mark somewhere between 0 and 10 on your Wheel of Life for how you feel about your health.

Close family

What sort of a relationship do you have with your closest family? There are lots of different ways you can measure that, but let me give you a couple of examples. Do you have the type of relationship where everybody just really cares about everybody else? Everyone is concerned about the other's needs and making sure things are just right for them?

Do you remember the old TV programme, *The Waltons*? Those guys lived on a mountain in a big white house and everything appeared to be perfect. Who could forget 'Goodnight John-Boy, goodnight Mama'? *The Waltons* is guaranteed vomit-inducing TV these days, but to have that type of relationship, where you can live with people and have total respect for who they are, where they want to be, to give each other the freedom to move, to grow, to give true unconditional support, then that's a real close family relationship.

Or do you have the type of relationship where you think, 'Christmas is coming soon, sod the lot of them. They are getting nothing this year. And as for my brother, well he was supposed to ring me and he didn't, so I'm not ringing him. Yes, I know it's been ages since I visited my Mum, but you know it's the same distance both ways. I know she's 96, but there *is* a bus'?

If your relationship with your close family isn't what you think it should be; if you have kids and are not communicating with them in the right way; if your 'significant other' isn't making you feel significant or vice versa, then I want you to give yourself a really honest score. You might be lucky; you might score high. Or maybe you are not so lucky and you know there are some challenges. The good news is, we are going to tackle those challenges in this book, so give yourself an honest score for your close family now.

Money

Yes – the dosh, cash, spendies, the readies. First the good news. It's not about how much money you have; it's about your relationship with money. You might be the type of person who, no matter how much you earn, still suffer from 'too much month at the end of the money!' (I've met many people who suffer from this.) Your idea of a financial strategy is to apply for a Visa card, and use it to pay off your Mastercard, and then you are going to get a new AMEX card to pay off your Visa card, and then you are going to get some store cards so you don't have to spend your money for a few months. Then the whole thing is going to build and build and build, and you are going to have a look at how many payments you've got to pay each month rather than how much money you're going to save. Then it's time to call a finance company to consolidate it into 'one easy payment' before starting all over again. Since the first edition of this book we've discovered governments using this method to manage their country's finances!

That type of financial management does not get you high marks on the money spoke of your Wheel of Life.

Think very carefully about your finances. Perhaps you're the type of person who knows exactly where your money is going each month. You have a financial strategy in place. You have an understanding of how money works. You know that if you do ever need to borrow money, you will have a strategy for paying it back that is completely within your means. You understand at any time where you are financially. But most importantly, you feel comfortable about money. Your relationship with money means that you understand it's always going to come in, it's always going to go out. That type of thinking and action gets higher marks. Whichever way you look at it, be very honest with marking this area of life.

I agree **money isn't** the most important thing in life. However, **many of the most important** things in life are often **made easier** by your management of money

Relationships

What type of friend are you? What type of work colleague are you? Think about the people with whom you are closest on a daily basis, and think about how they treat you. Imagine you are walking along the corridor and you see a group of people having a chat. They suddenly catch you out of the corner of their eye and they say, 'Oh oh, it's him, shhh!' You walk up to them and say, 'What's going on?' and you know they were talking about something that they don't want you to hear. Immediately your mind starts to play all sorts of tricks. 'Were they talking about me?' 'Were they organizing an event that I'm not invited to?' Well, there might be a reason for that. Is it because you are the type of person whose idea of strictest confidence is only telling people one at a time? If you're the type of person who thinks 'Well, you know, I've got to get myself absolutely sorted out first, and other people well, sod them, they can catch up later', I'm afraid you get a lower mark with this part of your Wheel of Life.

Or are you the type of person who really is a superb friend? The type of person who when friends or colleagues have a challenge or a problem they come to you, not just for sympathy, not just because you are going to be a shoulder to cry on, but because you give great advice? You have an absolute understanding. You have a level of care and passion that attracts people to come to you to be understood. If you are that type of person, it's great news because you get a higher mark here. So give yourself a mark for relationships on your Wheel of Life.

Contribution

If 'the secret of living is giving', then how would you measure your contribution? I'm not necessarily referring to financial contribution to worthy causes (although you may want to measure your contribution in that way). Contribution is about giving your time, resources, energy and spirit without expectation of anything in return.

Are you thinking of ways to make your society better or complaining that things aren't what they used to be? Do you give first without any expectation of what may be received, or do you like to receive first, then you're happy to pay back? You know the drill. Give yourself an honest mark.

Vision

Do you have a plan? Know exactly where you're going? On waking, do you have a clear objective for the day? Yes? Doesn't it make you feel great? What about in one year's time? What about five years? What about 10 years? What's your vision? Do you know exactly what you want to do? Do you know exactly what you want to achieve? If you're that type of person, you're going to get a high mark for vision.

I heard a great story once about Neil Armstrong. It goes like this. One day Neil Armstrong stood and looked at the moon and he said to his mother, 'One day I'm going to go there.' Everybody laughed. They would: he was less than 10 years old and there he was, telling people that one day he'd go to the moon. Space travel didn't exist at that time, never mind travelling to the moon.

Of course he continued with his amazing vision. He studied, he worked hard, and he became a test pilot. He was getting closer and closer, pushing the limits. Then he got a chance to join the Space Program. When the Lunar Program was launched, he was one of the very first to enrol. He worked tirelessly every single day, always making sure that he was at the forefront, continuing with 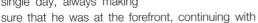 his vision. Of course, we all know what happened next. He got the chance to go to the moon, and not only that, he got the chance to be the first person to walk on the moon.

That level of vision, that level of passion and enthusiasm for a clear future is what drives many people. You're going to read a lot more about this throughout this book – about your vision, about where you want to go.

Of course, you may not know what you're going to be doing for the rest of the day, never mind tomorrow, next week or in one year, five years or 10 years' time. You may ask, 'Who on earth could possibly know what they're going to be doing in five years' time?' There are too many problems out there – too many factors, too many things that you can't control. Is that your way of thinking? Unfortunately you get a lower mark. So give yourself a mark for where you stand with your own personal vision.

Career

Do you wake up on a Monday morning and shout, 'Yes, it's a work day!' feeling full of energy and excitement about going in to work? Do you love your job so much you would do it for free? Are you lucky enough to feel excited and passionate about your work and career? Then you're on a high mark.

Or, do you wake up on Monday mornings with, 'Oh well it's Monday, great news. That means it's Tuesday tomorrow, closely followed by Wednesday, Thursday, Friday and the weekend – and weekends mean ... no work'? Unfortunately, some people have a career that they totally dislike. 'I hate doing this.' It's tragic really, but if you know you're in the wrong job, that the thing that you spend most of your time doing is not the right thing for you, then I'm afraid you must give yourself a lower mark. More good news: later on in this book I'm going to show you some fantastic techniques to juice up what you do or to help you find the job that you want to do most in your life.

Give yourself an honest mark on the wheel to reflect your score on career right now.

Personal development

Are you the type of person who gets passionate and excited when learning about successful people's lives? Are you passionate about your own personal growth? Do you love to learn? Do you yearn to grow? Do you need to develop? Are you really excited about new things? About learning? About changing? About stepping up? About being a better person? Great news – you're going to achieve a high mark for personal development on the wheel. In fact, here's the brilliant news; you get 2 bonus points just by reading this book! It's important that you recognize you've already started the journey.

Ask yourself: 'What was the last thing that I read?' 'What was the last course I attended that I paid for personally?' This is *personal* development. The investment is in your time, in your resources, to take a programme like this and to step up. You make a choice to personally develop yourself, that's what makes the difference. We spend hundreds and hundreds of pounds on our cars, on our own personal appearance, on fabulous holidays. But the biggest return comes from investing your time, energy and resources in your own personal development. Invest in your own growth and you see huge benefits paid back.

Give yourself a mark for how you feel about your own personal development, not where you think (or hope!) it's going to be in a week's time, a month's time or a year's time; how you feel about it *now*, at this exact moment.

Your own Wheel of Life

The next stage in the Wheel of Life is to join up all those different pointers. See the example over.

If you have a perfectly round circle of 10s, I would like to meet you personally, shake you by the hand, buy you a drink and find out how you are doing it. There are very few people who, at this stage, have a perfectly round Wheel of Life. Most of us have a wheel that is in and out, pointy and disjointed. When you have that type of wheel, is it any surprise that sometimes life is a bumpy journey?

The whole purpose of the Wheel of Life is to identify where the challenges are now. If you gave yourself a mark of less than 5 in any of the eight areas, then we've got some work to do. This book is about addressing those areas now.

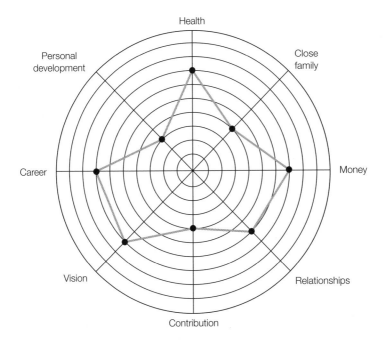

You may have been attracted to this book for one reason – to help with your career, say – only to find you have a mark of 3 for your close family. Whether your problem areas were clear or are a surprise to you, you're going to take actions to fix them right now with this book.

Or you may have a 10 in vision.

Ask yourself, 'What gives me that 10?'

What gives you that level of certainty about your vision that enables you to give yourself a 10? Could that vision help you in the areas of your Wheel of Life with lower marks?

The Wheel of Life, like most areas of personal development, is not something that you're only going to do once. The next stage is in one month's time, when you should prepare a new Wheel of Life, and repeat the process. Give yourself totally honest marks.

Take the first Wheel of Life you completed, along with your new one. Put one on top of the other, and hold them up to the light. You'll notice that in some areas you have improved. What have you done to achieve that? What actions did you take to change? It may be that another area of your Wheel of Life has started to drop slightly, it's not obvious immediately – but it's there, right in front of you. And that's what this is all about. The Wheel of Life allows you to focus on improvement; it's a continuous process, something to review every single month. It allows you to take action and fix problems before they become too serious.

If you need extra copies of the Wheel of Life then you can go to **www.michaelheppell.com** and print some from the resources section.

BRILL BIT

Work towards a balance to achieve a smoother ride in life.

This is a life-changing process for you. It makes such a big difference to the people who take the effort and make the commitment to fill in a Wheel of Life each month. You can do it more often if you wish. Go for balance. Remember – it isn't about getting a few 10s and ignoring the rest. It's about getting a wonderful balance.

I've been fortunate enough to meet some amazingly successful people; people who could have 20 out of 10 for career! Then they might have issues surrounding relationships or close family – areas where they need some help. I see people who have incredible methods for dealing with the area of money, or outstanding methods for dealing with health. Unfortunately they were so concerned about those areas that they ended up in the wrong job, they don't love what they do any more, and their life feels out of sync.

The Wheel of Life is about **getting a balance**; it's about personal growth; it's the foundation **to ensure** you have the **quality of life you deserve**

Truly brilliant people tend to have a brilliant Wheel of Life. But it doesn't happen by accident. They have a series of tools and techniques to use so that when they are applied, they become brilliant. They're called ...

TEN YEARS ON

Balance

The more I work with people around the world, the more I realize that this chapter contains the foundations to being brilliant. I want you to be brilliant AND happy. That's why the balance is so important.

A few years after writing *How to Be Brilliant* we wrote a book called *Brilliant Life*. The entire book is based on the sections within the Wheel of Life.

While writing *Brilliant Life* we asked our *How to Be Brilliant* readers which areas they found they had scored lowest in. The results were: (1) Contribution, (2) Vision and (3) Money. Last year we asked the same question. This time the results were: (1) Money, (2) Career and (3) Health.

I don't believe it's about how much money you have, it's more your relationship with money that you are scoring. Either way, money (lack of it and general concerns around it) is a much bigger issue today than it was 10 years ago. However, I also firmly believe that the opportunity to do something about it remains the same. But you must have a plan and you must stick with it.

It's also interesting that health has moved into the top three. The challenge to be brilliant in the important areas of your life is severely limited unless you enjoy vibrant health.

The good news is, for those self-inflicted health issues (overeating, under-exercising, etc.) you can gain 3 points on your Health spoke in only four weeks just by doing the right stuff right. How would that look on your Wheel? And how would that look in your mirror?

Just a final thought. What would you like your Wheel of Life to look like 10 years from now? Go on, fill it in.

My Wheel of Life 10 years on…

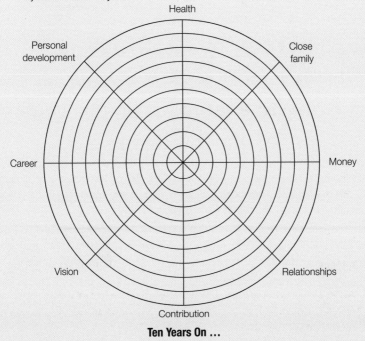

Ten Years On …

THE FIVE
CHARACTERISTICS
OF BRILLIANT
PEOPLE

speak at events all over the world and ask this question: 'Who do you consider to be brilliant?' The same names come up time and again. People who have truly changed the face of the planet, people who are renowned for their business success. Great sports people, great leaders and sometimes great friends or family members of the audience. When we start analysing exactly what it is that makes people brilliant, almost everyone agrees on the same set of characteristics. Here are the top five characteristics of the most brilliant people.

1 Positive action

Would you agree that the most brilliant, successful people in our society, actually the most brilliant successful people throughout history, are positive? Would you also agree that we tend to be a nation of moany-faced sods? Imagine if that was an Olympic event! Great Britain would win a guaranteed gold! Just imagine the medal ceremony, as our representative slouches towards the stage to receive their medal, looks at the first, second and third podium and says, 'Do you expect me to climb all the way up there?' After a bit of huffing and puffing the medal is placed. Our representative glances down, looks little bit disgruntled and says, 'Well, it's not very big is it?'

Why do we **behave in this way?** Perhaps society dictates we should. Maybe it's **simpler** to take the **negative route**

This is the point where you think I'm about to tell you all about positive thinking. Well no – I'm not. There's nothing wrong with positive thinking but I really do believe that it's *positive action*, more than positive thinking, that's important. In fact positive action is the number-one cornerstone to making a huge difference to the way that you live your life. Let me explain the difference. Positive thinking is great; yes, I'm a fan of it, but it doesn't work all the time. (Negative thinking – now that works 100 per cent of the time.)

American motivational speaker Tony Robbins describes positive thinking as like walking into a garden full of weeds, looking down and saying, 'No weeds, no weeds, no weeds.' What will it do to the weeds? Nothing. It's the *actions* that you take that make the difference.

Thoughts are things – it's the doing that makes the difference.

You can take this to an extreme. The next time you need to weed your garden, dress in a skin-tight *lycra* suit with a giant 'W' on the front and attach a flowing cape to the back. Take a golden trowel, play *The Eye of the Tiger* as loud as you can, and pace into your garden as 'Weed Man' or 'Weed Woman' shouting, 'COME ON YOU WEEDS … !' as you attack the weeds full on.

EYE OF THE TIGER

I guarantee, in no time at all, you will have got rid of the weeds, your neighbours, friends, family …

Or you might just fancy a bit of full-on weeding minus the costume!

So if you are agreed that it is the actions you take that make the most impact, what are the most important and the most common actions you carry out every minute of every day?

I was recently told that there are 1,250,000 words in the English language. 'Seems like a lot', I said, but I'm happy to accept it. Now let's take a look at how you use those words. The words you use in thought, the words you write, the way you communicate, the power of words. How often do you use negative language? Think about it. What is your stimulus response (your immediate involuntary action) when somebody asks, 'How are you?' You retort with words that seem to be embedded deep within us. You might say something like 'Fine' or 'Not bad'. Is that the best you can do with 1.25 million words to choose from?

Here's a 30-day challenge for you. When asked, 'How are you?' say (you've probably guessed by now) – *the best word* – 'Brilliant'. You may ask, why that is such a great word? Well, first of all, it's very emotive. Second, a word like 'brilliant' makes a difference as soon as you say it. The third thing is the reaction it gets from other people, especially if you have been a 'Not bad, thanks' person for years and years. Suddenly somebody says, 'How are you today?' and you reply with 'Brilliant! How are you?' That is when you start to get amazing responses. You might then be asked if you've just been to a seminar or if you are on drugs!

Believe it, *as you say it*. Sometimes it's a bit of a challenge because you may not really feel brilliant. Wouldn't it be great if, for the next 30 days, no matter how you feel, no matter what's going on in your life, if somebody says to you 'How are you?' you reply 'Brilliant, thank you!'?

BRILL BIT

When you learn new responses, or any new language, you create a new pathway of brain cells. In this case the new pathway of cells is the 'Brilliant' pathway. The more you say it, the easier it becomes and the pathway strengthens. Brilliant!

Later on you'll discover how your brain works and understand what a key ingredient language is.

For now, use the 'Brilliant' response and you will see something amazing over the next 30 days.

BRILL BIT

The 'Brilliant' response tool will affect the lives of those around you. Watch as eyes light up when you smile and give a full-on 'Brilliant'. Use it when the skies are cloudy, the traffic is slow, the boss is going mad and the kids are driving you round the bend!

It doesn't stop there, because your choice of words, your choice of language, is vital for achieving brilliance. I'm not one of those people who walks around spouting, 'Yeah, yeah, yeah. Everything's wonderful. Everything's brilliant. Ooh, the world is a wonderful place' because sometimes it isn't like that. I am a true believer and really passionate about choosing the right words to describe the current situation.

Have you ever heard people say:

'I'm bored.'

'I can't be bothered.'

'I feel ill.'

'I'm tired.'

When you say things like that, guess what starts to happen? You start to become those things. You'll start to feel tired. You'll feel bored. If you say, 'I feel ill' then your brain has a process that will make you feel worse.

If I were teaching a group in California it would be really easy. If you felt tired you would say, 'Don't tell people you're tired, tell them you're ENERGIZED!' Stop for a moment and think what would happen if you did that where you live!

So what can you do? How can you change what you say without feeling that you're faking things?

If you are tired, would it be true to say you could actually 'do with more energy'? And would it also be true that your body has that energy? I sometimes challenge people on my live events, 'You may feel like you have no energy left. But if I was to challenge you that the first person to burst out of those doors, run twice around the block and get back in their seat will be given £10,000 cash, then I can guarantee that people who'd never run for years could find the energy to go out and have a crack at it!' The energy would materialize because it was always there, you just have to ask for it.

So, rather than say 'I'm tired', you could say 'I could do with more energy.' It may be a different choice of words to say the same thing but the result will be very different.

Let's take a look at the response that you're going to get from your brain when you say 'I could do with more energy': the key words here are 'more' and 'energy'. It's a direct request to your brain for 'more energy'.

Your brain is like a filing cabinet; it **references** every time you use a **particular word**

BRILL BIT

The more you use a word or sentence, the stronger the pathway of brain cells becomes. That's going to make a difference to how you communicate using your physiology, your facial muscles, your language, how much your eyes are going to light up, and how people are going to feel towards you. They're all going to make a difference.

When *you* say things like, 'I could do with more energy', immediately your intellect goes, 'Yep, I know how to do more energy.' Your amazing brain will release chemicals, it will change your breathing habits, you will stand in a different way – all because you will have instantly been given more energy.

If you are the moany type you might say, 'Well I'm quite happy feeling tired.' Great! If you want to do that, if you want to go through your life feeling tired and run down, then that's up to you. This is a language for people who want to change. This is a language for people who want to be brilliant.

Rather than say, 'I'm bored', why not say, 'This could be more interesting'? You don't have to turn it around and say, 'This is the most incredible, wonderful and interesting thing ever.' I repeat, you do *not* need to do that. What you do, very simply, is to say, 'This could be more interesting.' What do you think is going to happen if you say 'This could be more interesting'? Do you think you may find just something in there, just a small shred of evidence to show that the thing that you are listening to, that you are watching, that you are participating in *is* more interesting? Absolutely!

Bonus 30-day challenge

Have a real, what I call, 'pity party'. Write down the different types of negative language that either you hear yourself saying or you hear from other people around you. Write them down. Remember the learning is in the doing, so really do this exercise.

Now, with your list, here is what you must do.

Have a look at what is the opposite of the language that you are using. Before, when you said you were 'tired', could the opposite of that be 'energized'? When you were 'bored', could the opposite of that be 'interested'? If you said you 'feel sick', could you 'be healthier'? Explore the different types of language.

The next step is to say, 'OK, we aren't going to go over the top here, I want brilliant results but what would the truth be?'

Sometimes people feel a little bit run down. Therefore if you want to continue to feel run down, just start telling people that you are feeling run down. If you want to feel better, say, 'I could be feeling healthier.' You can do this with some integrity. Say it like you mean it, like you really do want to feel better. Guess what starts to happen? Very very quickly, you'll start to feel better.

> If you **want** more energy and you say
> 'I could **do with** more energy', then
> you'll soon be **given** more energy

Here is a list of some classics and some new language for you to test:

I'm tired	I could do with more energy
I'm bored	This could be more interesting
I'm really hacked off	I could be happier
The weather is awful	The weather could be better
I'm scared	I could be more confident
This is crap	This could be better
He's a liar	He could be more truthful

I'm freezing	I could be warmer
It's too hot	It could be cooler
I'm broke	I could do with more money

Sometimes though this doesn't work – sorry, could work better! In some areas the next positive action is to use the *power of questions*.

What questions are you asking yourself? What are you saying to yourself every single day? What are the questions going through your head?

Sometimes we say, 'Why is this so boring?', 'Why does that happen?' or 'We can't change this'. What if you were to say things like, 'How could I change this?', 'How could this be more interesting?' Ask a different question – you get a different result.

BRILL BIT

Questions are so powerful. When you ask yourself a question your brain has to answer it. It might not think it knows the answer straight away, but it starts to process finding an answer and the answer will come.

You have to be very careful about the questions you ask. First, make sure they are positive. Make sure that they are going to demand a response from you. When you ask those questions of yourself, again and again, in a positive way, I guarantee you'll get positive responses coming back through.

Sometimes when I hold seminars people say to me, 'Yes, I'm going to do that. I'm going to try and be more positive. I'm going to try and use this language.' They even write down 'I'm going to try harder, I'm going to try to find a way.' There is a word in there that is a very disempowering word; that word is 'try'.

Here's an example. Wave your hand right now, just take your hand and start to wave it. I know it seems silly but go with me on this. If you are reading in a public place you might make some new friends! So go on, wave your hand for a moment. OK, stop. Don't wave your hand at all. Keep it still. Now try and wave your hand – go on, try and wave your hand. If your hand has moved, that's not trying – that's waving your hand like the first time. Just 'try' and wave it. As you see, 'trying' to do something is the same as not doing it.

'Try' is a **weak** word

BRILL BIT

If you ever organize a party and someone says, 'We're going to try and be there' then put them on the 'We won't be there under any circumstances even if it was the last party on the planet' list. When people say 'try', it's a wimp's way of saying they are not 100 per cent committed to doing something.

So now you know that you can change your language; you can change your stimulus responses; you can ask better questions; and there are other words you can eliminate altogether. The final part of this important section of the book is your self-talk. What do you say to yourself? It's very simple to put yourself down. 'Why can't I do this?', 'I'm so ugly', 'I'm too fat', 'Why am I so stupid?', 'It doesn't work for me', 'Nobody likes me', etc. Of course the more that you do this, the more you believe the self-talk, and the more you will start to become like the language that you use. So your self-talk is critically important.

Who controls self-talk? You do. Sometimes it feels a little bit uncomfortable when you have been beating yourself up for so long to suddenly turn around and be a more positive person. Sometimes it feels like you are faking it. Well, that's OK, because initially you may have to feel that you are faking some of your self-talk, by starting to tell yourself that you are doing well, telling yourself you are popular, and saying internally and externally that you do feel good about yourself. The more that you tell yourself these positive affirmations, the closer you get to being that type of person.

Yes, it starts with the language that you use. I'm not saying that you should turn around and yell, 'Yee-ha, everything in the world is wonderful, the sun always shines and it's a most incredible place ever and everything is superb to me, raa-raa-raa-raa-raa', because people like that could get locked up! All I am suggesting is you can choose how you feel about each given situation and use your language to reaffirm this.

BRILL BIT

The first characteristic of being a brilliant person is to take positive actions. Be positive with the words you choose, the questions you ask and the internal language you use.

2 Break out of your comfort zone

The second characteristic of brilliant people is that they break out of their comfort zones. Things that hold other people back they just seem to smash through. And they don't just do it once, they do it again and again.

I heard a great story once about two friends who were at school together. One of them was called Richard and the other one was called John. Richard and John had a plan to start their own school magazine. They talked about it and they talked about it. It was easy just to talk about it, but one day Richard said, 'We're going to have to go and ask the head if it's possible to start our own magazine.' So they arranged to meet at midday and ask the head for permission.

They stood there waiting to go in and all of a sudden John nervously said, 'I'll be back in a moment' and he rushed off down the corridor. After five minutes he hadn't returned so Richard decided he was going to do it anyway. He took the first step out of his comfort zone and started to walk along the corridor.

This was an old-established, very traditional boys' school. As he walked along the corridor, past the portraits of previous heads and distinguished old boys, he felt butterflies in his stomach. He arrived at the end of the corridor and there on the door a brass plate announced, 'Headmaster's Study'. He knocked and after a moment or two the door flew open and there was the head, a very tall, very proud man.

At that point, I must say, Richard was frightened.

'Yes, what do you want, Richard?' boomed out the voice.

'Well, Sir, John and I were wondering' – no sign of John of course – 'whether it would be possible to start our own school magazine?'

'But we have a school magazine; it comes out each term.'

'Yes, but we want to do this a little bit more often, we want it to be fun, we want it to have jokes in. It's going to be great for our English and it's going to be a great skill for us to learn.'

The head agreed to it but the rules were: they had to produce it themselves; they had to pay for everything themselves; and they had to make sure everyone knew they were publishing it – high risk.

Richard left the office and found his friend.

'John, where did you go to? What happened? What happened to you?'

John sheepishly stammered, 'Well, I was going to come along, but I, well I, I just ...'

'It doesn't matter – great news – we can do it, but we have to pay for it ourselves, produce it ourselves and take all the risk.'

At that point John started, 'I can't believe it. Oh no, we are never going to get the money. How are we going to print it?'

'Forget that,' Richard said. 'Let's just write it – we can do it.'

They wrote the first edition of the magazine and managed to copy it with one of those old roller copier machines. They were so excited about it, all covered in ink and ready to distribute their work of art. They went in to school the next day and they started to hand out copies of their magazine. One sheet of A4 copied on both sides with all sorts of stories, little anecdotes, some poems and some fun.

Everybody who read it agreed on one thing ... that it was absolute rubbish. Richard and John found copies lying on the school field, pushed into the back of drawers and thrown on the floor. At that point John immediately jumped back into his comfort zone. But Richard thought about things differently. He asked a better question: 'What can we do to make this work?' They started to ask people good questions about what they would like to read, what they would be interested in. What they found was the things that they were writing about and what people actually wanted to read about were two different things. They went back to the drawing board and out of their comfort zones again. This time they produced a magazine that everybody loved.

Richard and John went on to produce another copy and another copy. Both boys were aged 16 and it came to the day that they left school. Richard had a suggestion for John, 'Let's start our own magazine.' John's response? 'I tell you what, let me think about it and I'll give you a call.'

He **never** called

Richard did start his own magazine. It was a magazine for students and it did pretty well. Sometimes he thought that it was going to go bust but within a year the team had built up quite a good readership. Richard noticed something; the people who were doing the very best from his magazine were the people who were selling things by mail order. It looked a great way to run a business; the money came in first – you bought the product at a discount and then sent it out. Brilliant! So Richard wanted to get involved with mail order and he decided to sell albums. He had never done it before, so once again it was a big step outside his comfort zone.

It seemed such a long time since he stood outside the head's study. That was easy compared to what he had to do now – setting up deals, buying albums – but once again his business idea was starting to really work. Who should he bump into but his old friend John! It was now two years after leaving school.

He said, *'John, I can't believe it's you. I'm doing so well. The magazine is doing great but I'm starting to get much more into this idea of doing mail order. We're advertising in other people's magazines and I'm too busy. Do you want to run the magazine?'*

John asked, *'Well, how's it going?'*

'Well, you know it could be better; cash is tight but let's go for it anyway. We'll be partners. Do you want to do it?'

Once again, John said, *'Richard, I'll give you a call.'*

He **never** called

Richard didn't worry for long; he was caught in a bit of a predicament. He had a lot of records and there was a postal strike. If he didn't sell that stock, he knew his business would go under. A friend of his suggested there was an opportunity to take a shop on Oxford Street in London above an old shoe shop. They filled it up with records, stood outside and dragged people off the street to go in and listen to the records, buy the records, chill out and have some fun. They did so well those first few days that Richard saved his business and he liked the idea of record shops. He quickly opened another one and then another two. But Richard noticed that the people who were doing really well from the music industry weren't the people who had the record stores; it was the people who owned the record companies.

So once again he moved out of his comfort zone and he started his own record company. Whereas everybody else was signing up a certain kind of act at that time, he signed a guy called Mike Oldfield. A funny little guy who had this great plan to record an album called *Tubular Bells*. Richard let him go completely crazy with it; he gave him a total free rein and he created something that had never been heard before.

Not only did Richard take a risk, but he took an amazing calculated risk because it became one of the biggest selling albums of all time, and that's a good start for a record company! Not only was he doing well with his other businesses but he was now involved with the record industry and started to expand things. Starting new businesses was easy for Richard now. He got involved with publishing, started to get involved with videos and video games. Business was easy and he needed another challenge.

Who should he bump into? His old friend John! Richard gave him one more chance, 'I'm about to start a new magazine, a brand new kind of magazine, and I want you to come and join me.' This was five years from when they left school. John thanked him for the opportunity and said, 'I tell you what I'm going to do, Richard. I'll give you a call.'

He **never did** call

As you can probably guess, Richard went on to do many things, not only with his businesses, but he also started to challenge himself physically. He challenged himself to be the fastest person to get across the Atlantic in a boat. He also set a challenge to be the first person to fly across the Atlantic in a hot air balloon. The first time he failed. The second time he managed to do it. He set a challenge to be the first person to fly across the Pacific in a balloon. Do you remember the first attempt? I watched on TV as the balloon stood up and the sides started to peel off; it had frozen and when it stood up it all came to pieces. For a moment, if you saw Richard on the television, you'd think he wasn't a positive person! He quickly regained his composure after using the 'F' word – not fantastic, the other one – and he said, 'We'll be back next year. We're going to come back and we're going to do it again.'

Sure enough, one year later, once again massively out of his comfort zone, Richard attempted the flight again. This time Richard and his team succeeded. They were the first people to fly across the Pacific and, of course, he had a press conference. It was in a big sports hall in Canada, the world's media were there and it was beamed back live to the UK. It was being shown on BBC television that night. Somewhere that night there was a man sitting with his family who turned to his wife and he said, 'I could have been Richard Branson's business partner.' His wife turned to him, yawned and said, 'Yes, John, I know.' He must have told that story 1000 times about what could have been.

BRILL BIT

Who knows what would have happened if John had joined Richard in his business ventures? Who knows what sort of a lifestyle he would have enjoyed? Maybe it wasn't for him but he never gave himself a chance to find out. He'll never know. Why? He couldn't break out of his comfort zone – the thing that was holding him back.

So what is it that holds you back? What is it that keeps you inside your comfort zone? FEAR. It's fear that holds you back. Fear of failure. Fear of what people might say or think. Fear of getting it right then having to do it again. Fear of what you may lose. All these fears and many more hold you back. Think of fear as a simple acronym for:

False

Evidence

Appearing

Real.

Start by analysing situations when you've been too frightened to do something. Maybe it's been meeting a new person, an interview for a job, taking an exam, asking for a pay rise, communicating the benefits of a new product or a new service. These are moments when you feel anxiety. When you look back, what you thought you were frightened of and what you were really frightened of were two different things.

BRILL BIT

I guarantee if you begin to analyse your fears and the things that you really believe are holding you back now, you'll notice that 95 per cent of them you just made up. You created them. It was false evidence that you thought of or it was something crazy you believed that somebody else said.

Let's create some tools that you can use right now to overcome those fears, get out of your comfort zone and increase your confidence.

Here's a brilliantly simple way to get out of your comfort zone, plus you are going to make new friends and positively influence some other people's lives.

I would like you, in the next 24 hours, to start conversations with five people you've never met before, five complete strangers. Start talking to them. Make their day. Pay them a compliment. Find out something about them. If you're on the train, talk to the person who is opposite you. If you're on the bus, talk to the person who's sitting next to you. At the supermarket, talk to people in the queue, talk to the person sitting behind the checkout (they'll definitely welcome some stimulation!). Talk to someone in a lift. If I walk into a lift with more than two other people I usually say, just as the doors close, 'I suppose you're wondering why I called this meeting?' The reaction is great. If you can get smiles on their faces, you get bonus points for this process, but it must be five people in 24 hours.

You know what? You are going to enjoy it so much that in the next 24 hours you're going to do another five, and wouldn't it be great if that became a habit? Out there every day positively influencing people's lives by communicating with them. Do you know what's going to happen once you've talked to 50 people? You'll wonder why you were ever scared about communicating with strangers.

You might be reading this now and saying 'Well I do that already. That's the type of person I am.' That's great. Do it bigger, do it bolder and be better. Communicate brilliantly. Talk to the person who you would least expect to have a conversation with. If you go to a party, or to a function, talk to the people you normally wouldn't communicate with. Here's the really great news: confidence is transferable. You'll feel the benefits of this exercise in all areas of your life.

The next stage is to document times – actually write down and keep a diary of moments when you've broken through your comfort zone. You will know when you've broken through those limiting beliefs. Start keeping a diary so that if you get into a time again when you are worried, when you think 'Oh, no, what can I do about this?' then you can refer back to that diary and tell yourself, 'I've done this before. I know I can do it. Come on!' Use self-talk, use the positive language that we talked about earlier to make a difference for you.

Finally, if you really want to burst out of your comfort zone, use these three magic ingredients:

Pace, team and fun

★ **Pace.** Increase your pace. Physically move faster, do things quicker and you'll feel more confident about moving out of your comfort zone. Just think what you do when you are close to a deadline. You'll pick up the phone to anyone on the day of a house move if you haven't received the keys! Create a sense of urgency to help you out of your comfort zone.

★ **Team.** Work as a team. It's always easier to break out of your comfort zone if you're working with others who have the same beliefs as you. Imagine being part of an organization where it's the norm to be out of your comfort zone. Make sure that you are surrounding yourself with people who encourage you to go for it rather than playing it safe. If you want to know who you will be in five years' time, take a look at the people who you spend most of your time with and the books you read.

★ **Fun.** The third element is fun. It's much easier to be out of your comfort zone when you're having fun. I recently bought part of a company and sold part of one of my companies and had some big meetings with lawyers. At the end of the meetings, the partner in the lawyers' firm commented on the fun we'd had in the meetings and how unusual this was. 'Most people just sit and worry' he told me.

BRILL BIT

Don't be most people!

3 Think differently

A key characteristic of all brilliant people is that they think differently. If they had the same thinking process as other people, then they'd get the same results. I love this quote from Einstein:

> *'You can't solve your problems with the same thinking that caused them in the first place.'*

Isn't that wonderful?

Understanding how your brain works is the first stage towards having a different way of thinking. Understanding the processes that take place will make a difference.

Many people have talked about left and right brain thinking. I first read about it over 20 years ago and I got a closer understanding when I started to study the work of personal development geniuses and psychologists around the world. The first thing I grasped was that the brain has two main hemispheres. They form the neo cortex, which means new cortex. It's the most recently formed part of the brain, and is the part that deals with most of your higher-order thinking.

In the 1960s, two guys, Robert Ornstein and Roger Sperry, did masses of research into the brain. They knew that the brain has processes on the left-hand side that control the right-hand side of the body, and processes on the right-hand side that control the left-hand side of your body. The Egyptians first discovered this whilst they were building the pyramids. People would get head injuries and whilst treating them they also discovered that the left brain was controlling the right-hand body and the right brain was controlling the left-hand body. Ornstein and Sperry discovered there was a different type of 'higher order' thinking going on in the two hemispheres.

Let me explain. The left hemisphere is responsible for mainly analytical types of thinking: logic, reading, sequence, speech etc. The right hemisphere, by contrast, processes artistic, musical, spatial awareness, imagination, rhythm etc. People frequently make the mistake of saying that the right-hand side of the brain is the creative part of the brain and the left-hand side is purely a logical part of the brain. This isn't true. Recent research suggests that the brain can actually use different parts in different ways and can simulate different types of thinking in different parts of the brain. Right now you're going to look at how you get the two parts working together because that is when you get true creativity.

Nature is a wonderful thing. You have a left leg and a right leg; a left arm and a right arm; a left eye and a right eye. The way they work best is together.

I don't know if you've noticed, but our education system starts off by being amazingly creative. Young children have a great balance of left-brain and right-brain activity. I remember when I was in primary school enjoying 'music and movement'. Super creative, leaping around the school hall – with just my underpants on! Or was that just my school? We used to do these wonderful artistic activities. Do you remember? 'I'm a lion, I'm a tiger, I'm a spaceman.' We would be so creative and so imaginative. Then things started to change and we began to believe it was stupid to think and act like that.

Our education system begins to put more pressure on being 'academically' (left brain) intelligent – more left brain, more left brain, more left brain – to the point where we start to measure somebody's 'intelligence' by how good they are at using their left brain. Ultimately, we leave our education system with a wonderfully developed left brain and an under-developed right brain. You would never do that with another part of your body, would you?

Can you imagine starting up the treadmill but running with just your right leg? 'I'm just doing my right leg tonight.' 'Just my right arm on the weights today, build up that right body.' You would end up with a really strange looking body if only one half of it was fully developed. So why do you do it with your brain?

How about thinking of things in a different way and focusing on getting a true balance? Left brain and right brain – working together. That's when you have true creativity.

Michael Flatley was the main source of inspiration behind *Riverdance*. I watched a TV programme where Michael talked about each degree of planning that went into creating the show. First of all, how he and his team had to measure the exact size of the stage, so that the ideas (which were in his head and had not been choreographed at that point) could be put into practice. The right-hand side of his brain, using this wonderful imagination, would be exploring how the dance might feel or look. The left-hand side of his brain would be working out the parameters in which people would move. Then the team had to think about and measure the exact area where people would be standing; understand the practicalities of getting changed in time between scenes; calculate how the music was going to fit; and ensure the finances would work for putting on the production.

BRILL BIT

Creativity comes when both sides of the brain work together.

The brain of three parts

How would you like to know more about your brain and how it works in 99.9999 per cent of the population?

Dr Paul MacLean came up with a wonderful theory about how your brain works and how it processes information. For me, this is very exciting because I got a real understanding about how we process information and thoughts. Dr MacLean talks about the 'triune brain', or the 'brain of three parts'. He shows the brain has three main areas.

The first area is called the reptilian brain. The reptilian brain is at the top of the spine and can only do basic functions such as a fight or flight response. In other words, 'Put 'em up', or 'Whoosh, I'm out of here'. That's all it's going to do. It was the earliest part of your brain to develop and it cannot do any 'higher-order' thinking: it cannot make creative decisions, it cannot remember things the way that other parts of our brain do but it does have some great uses.

I remember seeing Steve Irwin (RIP), the famous Australian crocodile hunter, when he went to catch a croc in this huge pond. He had to catch the crocodile because it had a septic foot. It was in a lot of pain and Steve wanted to catch it to treat it.

If it had been me, I'd have fired a dart from half a mile away and once the croc was fully unconscious, I'd get my full body armour on and with six big mates I'd go in with a metal net, wrap it up and drag it out. Not Steve Irwin. His plan was to walk in, feed it half a pig and then when it was sleepy after a nice big meal, jump on its back. Good thinking Steve! The guy was as mad as a box of frogs! I really love the way that he worked, but his commentary for this task was the most exciting part.

As he walked into this swamp with half a pig, he turned around to the camera crew and said, 'Well, she's in here somewhere, mate. She's an absolute beauty this one but because she's got a really poorly foot, she's going to be a bit grouchy.' I'm thinking 'Going to be a bit grouchy!' Then he goes on to explain how this crocodile is about 4.5 metres long and has amazingly powerful jaws that could take your leg off in one move.

As he's getting deeper and walking further into the swamp, I suddenly realize that with him there is a camera crew. Two guys were there filming it, but who was looking after them? What would happen if suddenly the croc leapt out? I'm sure the cameramen had the same thought because there was a little bit of camera shake!

Steve's now going deeper and deeper and getting more excited and he's explaining how the croc can smell blood at 50 metres. The camera swoops down on to the pig and there it is dripping with blood. Suddenly they see some movement out of the corner of their eyes and the camera turns around and just at that point this crocodile is coming towards them and Steve throws the pig right into the jaws of the crocodile but she avoids the pig and goes for them! They start running at that point – they don't want to be hanging about. They run about four or five steps but then they have to jump over a 2-metre fence! In one bound all three of them leap. Moments of relief and heavy breathing later they realize they're safe. Looking back, what was it that gave them the power to move so fast and leap the fence?

It was during that time of 'flight or flight' that the reptilian brain was able to release adrenalin and cortisol into their bodies to give them the energy and the power to get out of there. You don't want to be using the creative part of your brain at that point. You don't want to be thinking 'Isn't it wonderful that this animal has been around since prehistoric times. Isn't it fascinating how each one of those teeth has hundreds of pounds of pressure that could just tear your leg off in a second?' You don't want to be doing that; you want to be out of there and fast. Escaping from a crocodile? That's a great use of the reptilian brain.

What about bad use of the reptilian brain? It could be having an argument with your partner, perhaps being stuck in a traffic jam, or when you receive a bad piece of news and think, 'I wasn't expecting to get that.' Suddenly all hell can break loose, as people start using their reptilian brains to deal with the situation. This is *not* good for you. Adrenalin that goes into your body, unless it's used, say, to get out of a dangerous situation, is going to stay. It's going to manifest and cause health problems and stress. I get concerned about this because I know that if people aren't using that adrenalin to get out of a high-danger situation it can become evident in all sorts of ways: heart disease, strokes, cancers. You don't want that.

So get conscious about the way you use your brain.

Be aware of the times when you might **'go reptilian'**

How do you choose which part of your brain to use? The neuroscientist Paul MacLean talks about the central part of the brain, or the mid-brain, which is also known as the limbic system. The limbic system processes information such as long-term memory, emotion, habits, your behaviour. In fact, this is the part of the brain that makes you who you are. Your personality and your traits are in the limbic system. And it's your limbic system that filters thoughts.

A thought may come into your head and you have to decide, which way will that thought go? The thought or stimulus goes in to your limbic system where your long-term memory, your emotions, your habits, your behaviours, the things that make you who you are, are housed. The limbic system then asks, 'Am I going to send the thought up to the neo cortex, to the creative, imaginative part of the brain? Or am I going to send it down to the reptilian brain, the part that's going to snap, the part that's going to react, the part that's just going to run away from the problem, escape from the challenge or fight against it?'

It makes that decision at the speed of light. So how can you make a difference to the way your thoughts are processed? Simple.

Train your brain

You may now be thinking, how on earth can I train my brain when the thoughts are being processed at almost the speed of light?

It's very simple. Start with the small ones. Remember your response to 'How are you today?' When you choose to say 'Brilliant', you're already training your brain for a more positive result. You are creating a habit of sending your thoughts up to the creative, imaginative neo cortex. When a situation comes along that is more threatening or serious, your brain is more likely to send your thoughts upwards to the neo cortex. Why? Well it's used to sending the thoughts that way, every minute of every day.

BRILL BIT

Imagine a football team. They practise every single day. They practise passing the ball to the midfield players. All they do is kick the ball back to the defenders. The defenders don't do anything with it; they just knock it around to the back of the pitch.

Now it's 3 o'clock on a Saturday afternoon, the whistle blows and the game starts. Which way is the ball going to go? The ball is going to get kicked back to the defenders, because they practise all week doing that. They don't know any other way; a bit of a boring football match plus it's a match that that team is going to lose. But what if they practised another way every day? When the ball goes to the midfield players, the midfield players practise kicking the ball to the strikers. The goal scorers are situated where the exciting part of the game is taking place. Those people are the ones who are going to win.

So, the midfield players are the limbic system. The defenders are the reptilian brain. The goal scorers are the neo cortex, the creative, imaginative part of the brain. By choosing which way you send your thoughts on a consistent basis you can train your brain to deal with different situations in a much more positive and imaginative way.

Now that you know this, you have joined a very small percentage of the population who understand how their brain works. There's now evidence from MRI scans that when people are given the same stimulus, they deal with the information in their brains in different ways. I watched a video of two people: one was a moaner, the other was a very positive person. They did scans of their brains as their thoughts were taking place. With MRI scanning, you can actually see the brain lighting up as it thinks. The positive person, no matter what information they gave him, dealt with it using his neo cortex, the thinking cap, the creative and imaginative part of the brain. The moaner, no matter what piece of information they gave him, dealt with it using his reptilian brain. With the same information, processing it in two different ways, which one do you think had the better quality of life?

One of the challenges of changing the way we process our thoughts is that it all happens so quickly. By the time you've given a negative response or reacted in a particular way it's over. Or is it?

Take 2

Actors fluff their lines and often cinema shots don't look right. The magic of the movies means they can simply say, 'Take 2' and do it all again. Here's a thought. So can you! When you catch yourself being negative, rather than thinking 'It's too late', just give yourself a chance to Take 2 and relive that response again.

I know as a parent I would say 'No' to my kids before they'd even finished a sentence! By using Take 2 you give yourself another chance.

'Mum, can I watch TV?'

'No! You can tidy your room ...'

Now you've caught yourself being negative, simply say:

'Take 2. Let's look at this in a different way. Yes, you can watch TV so long as you have tidied your room and done your homework.'

You don't have to say 'Take 2' out loud – but if you can it will help you to reprogramme your brain faster.

BRILL BIT

You use your brain in many different ways. The more you can train your brain to use the neo cortex, the thinking cap, the easier it is to process information and to get creative output. So, choose how you process your thoughts now to get the results you want.

4 Ability to manage stress

The next characteristic of brilliant people is their ability to manage stress. They actually turn stress into energy.

Stress is an unavoidable consequence of life. As Hans Selye (the endocrinologist who coined the term as it is currently used) noted, 'Without stress, there would be no life.' It's your ability to manage stress that counts. And relaxation is at the forefront.

To get the most out of relaxation you need to understand what happens in your brain when you are truly relaxed. And please don't take this lightly, as practising relaxation is a key ingredient to being the brilliant person that you deserve to be.

Let's start by looking at how your brainwaves work. Right now, when you are wide awake, your brain is functioning at a level that is known as beta. When you start to unwind you get to a place where you feel very relaxed and very calm: your brainwaves are now functioning at alpha. As you go off to sleep, you'll go first of all into a light sleep. That is known as theta, and then when you go into a deep sleep this is called delta.

The point where you're at your most relaxed, when you can completely rejuvenate yourself and also be incredibly creative, is between alpha and theta. That area, which is known as *alpha–theta*, is the point you want to aim for. Many are able to do it very very quickly, very very simply. Many who practise meditation are able to go there immediately. For most people though, it takes practice.

Beta – Wide awake

Alpha – Very relaxed

———————————————

Theta – Light sleep

Delta – Deep sleep

BRILL BIT

Thomas Edison, the greatest inventor of all time, would sit in front of his fire holding a large steel ball. The fire and comfortable chair would help him to relax, but if he relaxed too much, he'd drop the ball and wake up. He taught himself to hold his brain at alpha–theta and thought of many wonderful creative ideas at this point.

Some people say to me 'Oh yeah, I'm great at relaxing. When I'm stressed I switch on the TV. When I sit down in front of *EastEnders*, I chill out and feel so relaxed.' And when you think about it, you may be relaxed in that you're sitting down, you're not thinking about too much – and let's face it, most TV you don't have to think about. However, to truly rejuvenate yourself, you need to be in a place that gives your brain an alpha–theta type of relaxation.

Just for reference – **watching** TV is not **relaxing**

I often hear people make up all kinds of crazy stuff about stress. 'I actually work better when I'm stressed.' 'A bit of stress makes me feel great.' They get mixed up with *ustress* (excitement perhaps before a big event, roller coaster ride etc.) and *distress* (linked with panic, deadlines, worry etc.).

Let me tell you a story about an organization I was working with – a marketing company. It was a great organization but the head of this company had a belief that employees worked better when they were 'a bit stressed'. There was a great atmosphere in the office, people could do all sorts of things during the day, but he expected that when a deadline situation came along, they had to pull out all the stops and everyone would stay behind, up their pace and work rapidly towards hitting the deadline. All that would actually happen was that people would work faster. They weren't working any better. They weren't being more creative. They weren't being more imaginative; they were just working faster. I believe that it's a fallacy to think, 'I work better when I'm stressed.' No, you work faster. Sometimes you can get some adrenalin, sometimes you can get a buzz, but ask yourself: is that conducive towards achieving what you really want to achieve?

So it's very simple. To tackle stress you must find a way, every day, to relax to the alpha–theta level. Listen to a relaxation CD or download. Learn to meditate. Do yoga. Walk in the woods and choose not to think about anything. Learn to rejuvenate so that rather than getting stressed you give your brain an opportunity to understand information, process it carefully and then you get mega creative.

5 Massive action

The next characteristic of brilliant people is that they take massive action.

Would the people that you judged as being the most successful, as being the most brilliant, sit around and wait for opportunities to show up? Do you think they follow the crowd? Or are they leading the way by making things happen? My observation is that they are the ones who are out there taking massive action every day.

I sometimes have really lively debates with other trainers or people from organizations who say, 'Massive action is great, but we are interested in getting it right the first time.' 'Getting it right the first time' is a wonderful principle, particularly if you are an air traffic controller (I fly a lot!) or a brain surgeon. Sometimes, in fact for most organizations, my guess is that people would be much happier if they had a massive action atmosphere at work. Or a massive action atmosphere at play and a work environment where it was OK to sometimes make mistakes.

Why aren't **you getting** out there and **doing things** instead of just talking about it or **watching others** do it?

Procrastination

'I put the pro in procrastination. I'm great at it! In fact if that was an Olympic event I'd enter and win a gold. Not in the next Olympics though, I'll go for the one after that.'

Sorry for the bad joke – I couldn't resist it. However, the bit about me being a procrastinator is true. As it is for many people who struggle to find the motivation, the time or just something to make them actually start. If that's you, then read this next story carefully, as it may inspire you to take massive action and get massive results!

Picture this, Bill Gates being interviewed by Larry King on CNN. Larry King is really having a go at Bill Gates and forcing him to answer some pretty tricky questions. Bill Gates thinks he is let off the hook with an easy one.

'What's the secret of your success?' asks King.

'We were at the right place at the right time,' answers Gates. Of course, Larry King isn't happy with that answer.

'Well that's not true,' says King. *'Lots of people were at the place at the right time. But come on, you are Microsoft, you are the biggest on the planet at this stuff. What is it that you did?'*

'Well I guess we had a vision for the future for the home computer, for the desktop PC.'

'Yes, you had a vision,' King interrupts him, *'but yours was smaller than most of the competition. So come on Mr Gates, really what was it that made the difference?'*

'Well I think it must be down to the quality of our product.'

'It certainly isn't that,' King answers. Wow! By now Bill Gates is feeling a little bit uncomfortable, so Larry King pushes him one more time. *'Come*

on Mr Gates, what is it that really made the difference? Why is Microsoft number one? Why are you the biggest on the planet by far? Why do 90 per cent of PCs run Microsoft?'

Bill Gates turns and looks at him with total certainty and says, *'We are the ones who took massive action.'*

Larry King realizes he's finally on to something and he wants more. *'Can you give me an example of that?'*

Bill Gates shares a story about the time when they wanted to become the operating system for IBM and one day they got a phone call saying, 'Come down and show us the work you are doing.' They were there four hours later and that included a two-hour flight.

This was not a group of people who were hanging around. They immediately got on a plane and flew down there and spent as long as it took with the people from IBM. Of course, history shows that because they became the operating system for IBM personal computers, they continued to go from strength to strength, becoming the biggest on the planet.

Massive **action** = massive **results**

BRILL BIT

Never have any more than five items on a to-do list. Make them *must* do!

Even with those five characteristics, brilliant people have another ingredient that makes them leaders in their field, they practise ...

TEN YEARS ON

Brilliant

I've challenged literally hundreds of thousands of people to go for the 30-day programme of responding with 'Brilliant' whenever they are asked, 'How are you?'. The results for those who do it are amazing.

Teachers have gone from loathed to loved, doctors have been praised by patients and even the dullest chief executives have made their companies smile.

You must test this idea. Just do it for 30 days and you'll experience a noticeable difference. Let's start right now.

How are you today?

Branson

A couple of years ago I met Sir Richard and, in the spirit of getting out of my comfort zone, I shared with him how the story about John was a great way of showing how you have to challenge your fears. When I asked him if it was true, he gave me a Branson smile and said, 'More or less'.

I'll take that, as the person who told it to me added a pinch of poetic salt. The point is, when I ask an audience, 'Who do you consider to be highly successful – from any area of life?', Richard Branson is still the number one name on the list.

What have you learned about what he's achieved? And why (10 years on) is his still the name people associate primarily with entrepreneurial success? Personally, I believe his name comes up so often for three reasons:

1 He's a shameless self-publicist. And there's nothing wrong with that. He's sacrificed anonymity and set himself up as a target for the knockers. But it's amazing how many don't.

2 He likes having fun. I think we're all a bit jealous of Sir Richard's adventures and lifestyle.

3 He's a risk-taker. If you don't want to take risks you can still get a kick out of watching others take them. Setting up missions into space, taking on Coca-Cola, flying balloons around the world and a hundred other ventures have made him one of the world's best-known risk-takers.

Brains

As fast as you write 'the latest' information about the brain and how thinking takes place, it's been superseded by something even more amazing. Since the original publication of *How to Be Brilliant*, the following has been discovered:

★ You have a finite amount of willpower each day because to exercise your willpower you need energy in the form of oxygen and glucose. That's why it's harder to say 'no' when you are tired or not feeling yourself.

★ The hippocampus, which is the part of the brain that deals with visual–spatial awareness, is larger in London taxi drivers than normal people. This is due to the months, sometimes years, they spend learning literally every single street in the UK's capital before they are granted a licence to be rude and unsociable. Sorry, I mean take you by the best route to your destination.

★ You have something in your brain called mirror neurons. If you see somebody stub his toe, for example, the same pain area will light up in your own brain, causing you to flinch.

★ Your brain doesn't record memories like a video, as it would be easy to assume. It takes snapshots of the more important bits and then, when you recall the event, it guesses what happened in between, based on prior experience and generalizing.

★ Research is now suggesting that a 'gut instinct' can literally be a gut instinct, and that there is a mini-brain operating inside your stomach.

Almost all of these ideas came from Tim Brownson's wonderful eBook, *70 Amazing Facts About Your Brain and Why It Does Weird Things*, which can be accessed for free via his blog at **www.adaringadventure.com**.

3

BRILLIANT GOAL-SETTING

Time to set some goals. Already? But I don't know what I want! EXACTLY!!!

This is more exciting than you can imagine because you're going to do most of the work and see most of the results over the next 90 days. Ninety days is long enough to get some serious work done but it's short enough to see some results very quickly.

Let me share with you what I believe are the fundamentals of goal-setting. You'll have read in the introduction that I'm not a huge fan of SMART goals for creating passion and excitement. SMART (Specific, Measurable, Achievable, Realistic, Timescale) goals are great if you are doing project planning. But I believe the fundamentals of goal-setting start with a burning desire.

I want to talk to you about a more powerful goal-setting technique using the three Ps. The three Ps are very simple:

Personal

Positive

Present tense.

When you set goals, first of all they need to be **P**ersonal. Second, they need to be **P**ositive. Third, they must be set in the **P**resent tense.

When I say a goal has to be personal, it will include the big 'I'. Organizations can have goals, that's great. Shared goals for an organization are exciting; shared goals for a couple are stimulating; shared goals for a family are stirring; but right now we're talking about YOU – the most important person in the world – and what is going to make a difference to you and your life. Does that sound a little selfish? Maybe it's time for you to be a little selfish here.

BRILL BIT

When it comes to setting goals, you are going to tune into a radio station called WIIFM, that's:

What's In It For Me?

When you set a goal and write it down, it's going to start with the word 'I'. Such as – I am, I have. This will really help you to concentrate on what it is that's going to make a difference to *you* when you set your goals.

The second P is that a goal must be positive. I covered positive language earlier, so you should already have an understanding of how this works. Choosing the right words is absolutely critical at this point to make sure that you get the right affirmation created in order to achieve your goal. Let me give you an example. Once somebody said to me, 'I have my goal. There it is. What do you think of that, Michael?' They showed me their goal, which read, 'I am no longer in debt.' What's the key word in that sentence? It's *debt*.

You may be thinking, 'Why should that make a difference? That's a great goal. They want to get out of debt and they're being positive about it. It even sounds like it's in the present tense.' Positive language means that you would choose a different word (other than debt). The different words I suggested were 'financially free': 'I am now financially free', or 'I am financially free, now' – whichever feels best. 'I'm financially free' is much stronger and uses more positive language than 'I am no longer in debt.'

The third P is to set a goal in the present tense. See it as if it has already been achieved. This seems like a crazy idea to a lot of people and you may struggle to get your head around it. You may be thinking, 'Why would I do that? Could I not say, "One day I will be financially free" or "I will be financially free in two years' time?"' When you set a goal in the present tense, your subconscious starts working towards achieving the goal.

By setting **a goal in** the **present tense** you create **Gestalt**

Gestalt is a very powerful driving force that can change the speed at which you achieve a goal. Gestalt is your brain's way of wanting to create order. If you were to lie on the grass on a sunny day and look up at a blue sky and see the clouds rolling past, it wouldn't be long before you started to imagine other things those clouds might look like. You might say, 'Oh look, there's a ship' or 'Doesn't that one look like old Uncle Albert?' The reason for this is that your brain is making sense of a random image.

When you create a goal in the present tense, your brain says 'OK, if that's how things have to look, sound and feel, what do I have to do to make that happen now?' This is why a goal will happen so much faster if you set it in the present tense.

Here's an example of the person who I really believe was one of the greatest ever goal-setters – Muhammad Ali. Do you remember what Muhammad Ali would say? Do you remember the affirmation he would use? Four simple words:

BRILL BIT

What did Muhammad Ali say before he was the world champion?
'I am the greatest.'
What did he say when he was the world champion? 'I am the greatest.'
What did he say when he was no longer the world champion? 'I am the greatest.'
It's the perfect affirmation.

Think about the phrase, 'I am the greatest'. Is it personal? Is it positive? Is it in the present tense? Yes. Yes. Yes!

But to be the greatest, Muhammad Ali did more than just say he was the greatest. Ali would set goals in an altogether different way. Do you remember in pre-fight press conferences when he would turn to his opponent, look him in the eye and then make one of his famous predictions? Ali would say, 'You're going down in the second minute of the third round.' He would say it with such certainty and such belief that even though his opponent would say 'Yeah, right!', he knew that he was in trouble.

After the press conference, Ali would then do something very interesting. He would go back to his hotel room, or back to his home, lie down and relax from head to toe. In his imagination he would see the press conference just as it had been. He would see himself make that prediction, but then he would start to visualize the days and weeks ahead and see himself build up to the fight. He would see himself doing amazing training; he would imagine himself preparing and getting stronger and better than the other guy. He knew if his opponent was up at 5 am running, then he'd be up at 4 am. He envisioned himself during his sparring sessions, getting bigger and stronger.

Then he would imagine the day of the fight. He would arrive outside the stadium and when he got out of the car, the crowd would be chanting only one name. He would hear it repeated over and over again: 'Ali, Ali, Ali …' He would intensify the image. Increase the feeling. Bring it closer to him, imagining and feeling every single word, every single emotion that went with it.

Then he would see himself go into the dressing room and feel the bandages go on to his hands, he would feel the gloves go on and see himself standing strong. Then he would hear his name announced as he walks out. In his mind he senses the crowd going crazy, screaming just for him. Only his name would be screamed; everybody is on his side.

Then he would spring into the ring and look across the crowd, seeing every person screaming his name. He would hear it over and over again, intensifying it, increasing the volume, increasing the emotion: 'Ali, Ali, Ali, Ali'.

Then he would turn to his opponent and see him shrink small. They would touch gloves and begin to fight.

He would then visualize each round – mentally rehearsing the outcome he wanted. He would see the first round exactly as he'd planned it, exactly as he'd mentally rehearsed it. Connecting, brilliant blows, doing the famous Ali shuffle – float like a butterfly, sting like a bee!

Then he would visualize the second round, even stronger, even greater, intensifying every moment. Then came the third round and, more importantly, the second minute of the third round. At that moment – boom! He would connect with his opponent with an almighty punch, then see him go down. When his opponent fell, Ali would imagine standing over him and hearing the referee making the count – 'One, two, three, four, five, six, seven, eight, nine – you're out!' At that point, when he knew that he had won, he would freeze-frame the image and surround it in brilliant white light. He called this creating a 'future history'.

Never again would he consider an outcome other than his future history. All the time that he trained, he would see his future history. Every time anybody asked him about the fight, his future history was the image he would see. Every morning when he woke up, he would visualize his future history. Every night when he went to bed, his future history was the image that he would visualize. It was a future that he was so certain about, it was as if it had already been documented by the historians.

With that level of certainty, when it came to the day of the fight, you know what happened? His opponent would be knocked out in the second minute of the third round, exactly as he'd predicted.

That's how to set goals. Would Ali have been as successful if he had been taught to set SMART goals? 'OK Muhammad, make them specific, make them measurable, ensure they are achievable, realistic and with a timescale!'

Ali created a belief and a passion and brought it very much into his whole physiology so every moment he lived it, every moment he ate it, every moment he breathed it, every moment he felt it. With that level of certainty, and with that level of passion, you can achieve anything, anything that you put your mind to.

To create that level of intensity requires passion and a need to make a goal a 'must'. Here's your homework. Right now focus on the areas that are important to you. Think clearly about what exactly you want to achieve. To begin with, you're going to set some short-term goals. By this I mean things that are going to happen in the next 90 days. I also want you to have a look at where you want to be in one year; remember, that is only four batches of 90 days (see figure overleaf). Then think about where you want to be in five years and where you want to be in 10 years.

Ten years is a long time and the only limit should be your own imagination. Remember this brilliant quote from Michelangelo:

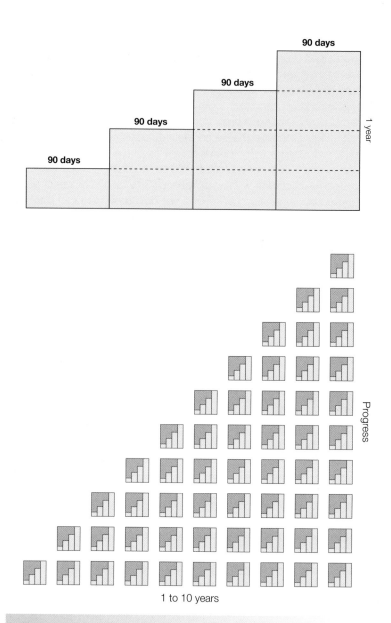

'The greatest danger for most of us is not that our aim is too high and we miss it, but that it is too low and we reach it.'

Think about that for a moment.

In 10 years you will have grown and developed massively. You could do whatever you choose to; you could be anywhere that you want to be. Just break it down into 90-day programmes, 90 days of doing the right actions. Do this and the 90-day chunks will start to build (see figure on p. 44). Your daily actions build up and you'll see yourself step up, step up so much that after three or four batches of 90 days, you're going to say: 'Wow. Look what I have achieved!'

It will be like a boat going through a lock system; every 90 days you get higher and higher towards achieving your goal. After 10 years you'll have travelled so high, you'll be amazed how far you have come.

So get practical and plan your first batch of 90 days. It won't always be easy, and some batches of 90 days will be tougher than others, but over time they will even out. After doing this, you'll see how easily you can plan your first year, the next five years and 10 years of this exciting new journey. Start by looking at the actions you have to take right now.

First question: which areas in your life do you want to set goals in? Remember when you first started to read *How to be Brilliant*, you looked at the Wheel of Life (p. 3). Eight different key areas in life. Some of the areas flagged up challenges where you knew you had to take action right now. They are the first areas to work on. Look carefully at your Wheel of Life. If you have a low mark in any area then you must set a goal there. It's an absolute must. The reason why? That area is holding you back – it's holding you back from getting the balance in your life that you deserve. A balanced wheel is the foundation. You will find it difficult to set big stretch goals later unless you have a balance first. So set some goals in each section of your wheel.

Do you have career goals? Do you have some areas within work where you say: 'Yes. I would really love to achieve that. That's where I want to be. This is how much money I want to be earning within my career. This is how many sales I want to be making. This is how many people I want to serve. This is the type of position that I want to have within this organization.' If so, you can create goals around your career.

What about within your relationships? What type of relationships do you want to have with people? Where do you want to be? How do you want people to view you? How do you want to be as a friend? How do you want to be as a partner? How do you want to be as a parent, an auntie, uncle, son or daughter? Could you have a goal in those areas as well?

What about your health? Do you want to make a difference to your health, to the way that you feel about yourself and the levels of energy that you have?

What about the things you really want? Do you want a particular car? Do you want to go on great holidays? Do you want to go and experience things that you could probably only have dreamt about?

Start to think about the things that really excite you, that really juice you up. Take a moment to write down a few ideas. Write down all the different things that come to mind with those areas. Think about the parts that might be missing from your life – what are they? How are you going to fill the gaps? Remember to raise your game here. Some are going to be short-term goals, others are going to be long-term goals. Stop reading for a moment and write a long extensive list. Go for it!

How not to write your goals

Here are a few mistakes people make when writing their goals and how you can avoid them:

★ Saying 'will' instead of 'have': e.g. 'I will sell my house' rather than 'I have sold my house'.

★ Using negative language: e.g. 'I am no longer in debt' rather than 'I am now financially free!'

★ Not making it personal: e.g. 'To have a cruise' rather than 'I am going on an amazing cruise'.

★ Not being specific: e.g. 'I have lost weight' rather than 'I have lost x pounds and weigh y – I look and feel amazing!'

★ Just writing the goals down then not taking any action towards achieving them. Goals without actions are only hopes.

Right now, you should have your list. And there will probably be too many things on the list, so read through them and ask, 'What do I *really* want?' You can identify the things that you *really* want because these are the ones where you can enthuse for hours about the reasons why and the difference they will make in your life. What are the things that are going to drive you as you look at your list? Then make sure you have a balance. To have goals only in one area of your life will quickly become unfulfilling.

Excellent. Now you have a list of goals written down that are positive, personal and in the present tense. You have made great strides in attacking the areas on your Wheel of Life where you had lower scores and you are beginning to formulate a 90-day plan to get a quick start on achieving your goals. You are heading towards brilliance rapidly. The foundations are laid, so if you are ready it's ...

Sorry, SMART

I was probably a little hard on SMART goals during the first page of this chapter. It's not that no one has ever achieved anything using SMART goals, it's just they're a bit ... dull.

As you've read, in this new edition I've rescinded my original statement about SMART goals and given them a bit more credit. If you are planning a project and want regular checkpoints to keep you on track during the life of that project, then SMART goals are pretty good. I'm just not sure they really inspire you to take action.

However ... if you want to jump out of bed on a Monday morning, bursting with energy and an attitude of, 'Yeeehaaa! Here's to another amazing week on my journey to achieve my brilliant life-changing goals', then stick with our three Ps.

A testing 10 years

I'm still a huge fan of 90-day chunks to get things done; I plan my whole life in blocks of 90 days. However, looking back, I do think the progress chart on page 44 showing nicely laid-out blocks of 90 days rising in a perfect slope to 10 years is a little unrealistic.

I think my and most other people's last 10 years would look a little more like this!

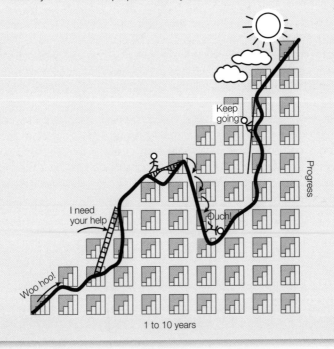

4

TIME TO BE BRILLIANT

When Sydney won the Olympics for 2000 it was an exciting time for Australia. A couple of years after the event I had an opportunity to work in Sydney and Melbourne. Particularly in Sydney, as I was meeting people, I realized that there was a unique energy and excitement in the air. People were excited about what was happening with their country. Businesses were booming. Tourism was going through the roof. I asked if they could put their finger on what it was that had made the difference. Several put it down to an exact moment: the moment when they actually knew that they were going to be hosting the Olympics in the new millennium.

I was fortunate to be introduced to the guy who was the Lighting Director for the Sydney Olympics and asked him about the Opening Ceremony. I don't know if you saw it, but at that time it was the most spectacular thing I have ever seen, for any event staged, anywhere. They had more colour, more excitement, more passion, more visual effects, more sound effects, better lighting and better fireworks. Everything was produced to the highest degree – it all came together amazingly tastefully and it worked so well.

I asked the Director about how they planned an event like this and what it was that made such a difference. He said:

> 'Michael, it started years before the event – all the people who were going to make it happen, the creative team, came together. The Chief Executive of the Sydney Olympics, Sandy Hollway, walked into the room. He looked at us and he said, "This is the brief for the Opening Ceremony of the 2000 Olympics. I would like you to get footage of every Olympics there has ever been. I would like you to obtain videos; I would like you to find books; I would like you to acquire photographs; I would like you to unearth old audios; I want you to interview people; I want you to find out what was it that made these previous events as exciting as they were. Then I want you to take the very best, the most exciting, the most emotive and the most passionate of each event. Then bring all that information together. Increase it to the power of 10 and that is your starting point!"'

My new friend concluded:

> 'Michael, we sat there with the hairs on the back of our necks standing on end. We knew we were about to create history. We knew that we were going to do something which had never been done before. We were so excited. For the next five years the excitement was just building all the time. We had to invent new technology to support our ideas. We wanted to do things that had never been done before and because of that excitement, because of that passion, because of that leadership, we were able to create an Opening Ceremony that has never been seen before. Not only that, but the whole Olympics continued to follow that same theme. We had the best transport system, it was the most organized Olympics for the athletes and the press, it was the cleanest, it had the best quality – everybody agreed that Sydney stepped up to the next level and created something which was truly brilliant.'

Why did it happen? How did it happen? Think about it! The days of doing a good job have gone. It is no longer good enough to be 'good' any more. When I work with a company I often start out by saying to their people 'I've done my research and the good news is that you're good.' The delegates will usually cheer here, but I continue, 'But there is some bad news. The bad news is you are good. And doing a good job just isn't good enough any more.'

Here's how brilliance benchmarking works. Let's stick with the Olympics and sport. Imagine a race is about to begin – the men's Olympic 100 metres. How much faster does the winner have to be than the second-placed runner to take the gold medal? In Athens 2004 the difference between first, second and third was one-hundredth of a second. In Beijing it was just two-tenths of a second and London just over a tenth.

Now, what sort of difference did that make to the first three athletes in the minutes, hours, days and months that followed? Well, the winner gets a gold medal. Oh, and millions of dollars in sponsorship, the opportunity to work with the best trainers and have the best equipment – and not forgetting the prospect of being able to run in any race meeting anywhere in the world. Everyone wants the Olympic champion.

Take a moment to think about the ones who came second and third. They missed out on a gold medal and all those rewards by a fraction of a second. They spent years preparing for that moment and missed it by a split second.

The good news is you are probably not an Olympic athlete. And that's good news because it means there is room at the top to be brilliant for everyone who reads this book, not just the gold medallist. But you have to know the rules.

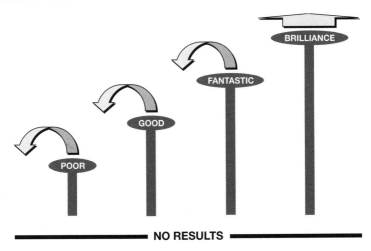

Take a look at the scale above showing the results people get versus the effort they put in. As you can see, on the base-line you have no results, nothing at all is happening. Just above that base-line you have a POOR job. Of course, if you do a poor job, the results you would expect to get would be poor. You don't want to do a poor job so let's go to the next level. The next level after poor is doing a GOOD job. As I said before, who wants to do a good job? Not me, because when you do a good job these days, what type of results are you going to get? No, not good! If only you were so lucky! You do a good job and you actually get POOR results. How do I know that? Because if you do a poor job you get NO RESULTS – you are out of business, redundant or barely surviving. Can you imagine if you were running a hotel, managing a restaurant or co-ordinating a mail order company and you were consistently doing a poor job, how long would you last? Not very long at all. So, if doing a poor job means you are out of business, it makes sense that by doing a good job you will get poor results. This can be a little disheartening but the examples are everywhere.

When I stay in a hotel, I walk into reception, check in, go to my room and the minimum I would expect is that the room should look absolutely immaculate. It should be clean. The towels should be neat. The bed should be made with well tucked-in sheets. The curtains should be symmetrical and the TV remote control should work. This is standard stuff. Not for a moment am I thinking that because this all checks out, they've done a great job. The minimum expectation I would have is that they would have done all that and more. Why? Because good is the minimum expectation of people these days. Your customers are expecting more and so are your family. So why do a good job when you end up getting poor results?

What is the next stage? The next stage is to go even higher than good (we were talking about this word earlier) by doing a FANTASTIC job. When you do a fantastic job, you would hope to get fantastic results, but look at the model. You do a fantastic job and still only get good results. Ah ha! Has the penny dropped?

Many people and organizations spend their time working somewhere between doing a poor and a good job. Every so often they peak towards fantastic. The results come back and they are only good, so what happens? They get disheartened and drop right down to where they were before, doing a good or a poor job. This can be frustrating for many people. You work so hard, do a fantastic job and still just get good results. Check your pay slip, are you getting paid too much?

I used to do a huge amount of work with charities, as my background was working as a fundraiser for several different organizations. They would tell me how they'd just had a 'fantastic' campaign. I would ask them, 'What was the purpose of the campaign?' 'We want to bring in money, we want to help people, and we want to do our work, so we need a lot of money in the organization.'

Then I would ask them the big question, 'How much money did you raise?' Often they would say, 'Well the results were good.' Then the organizations would start to justify good results by saying 'Think about the awareness that we gained for the organization. Think about the way that people viewed us.'

Yes, they did a fantastic job, but the money – the thing that they wanted to bring in that was going to change the organization, that was going to help their cause – was only good.

So, looking at that model, is there anywhere else you can go? There is and it is a tiny fraction; it's just a small difference. If you were to visualize it, it's only a few millimetres between fantastic and the next level, which is called BRILLIANCE! And that is the key to this book. True success and happiness is about not just doing a good job, not even doing a fantastic job; it is about doing a BRILLIANT job!

BRILL BIT

Brilliance is about pushing that little extra level, going just one further step, that extra mile. It's about caring more, understanding more, researching more, delivering more by putting in the effort that others don't and by achieving that you'll do a brilliant job.

Here's the most exciting part of the whole process. When you do a brilliant job you don't get fantastic results, you get brilliant results! The rewards are brilliant, the effect on others is brilliant, your quality of life is brilliant. I know it's not fair, but it's true.

If you understand the power of this concept, you'll immediately say, 'That's where I want to be. That's what I want in the important areas of my life.' You will want to do a brilliant job and receive brilliant results. However, the energy and commitment you have to put in to being brilliant is huge, so where you want results must be vitally important to you or you will not give the commitment, energy, passion and enthusiasm that will be needed to achieve brilliance.

When I first began to understand this concept I got very excited. Personally, I realized there were three main areas in my life where I wanted to do a brilliant job. Where being fantastic wasn't going to be good enough, where being good was just going to be shocking, and where being poor was a thought I couldn't even contemplate.

Firstly I wanted to be brilliant at being a Dad. I have two great kids and I realized that being a great Dad was going to be one of the most important things, if not *the* most important thing I could do in my life. The second was I wanted to be brilliant at the work that I do and the third was to be a brilliant husband.

Being a brilliant Dad

It's easy to say, isn't it? It is one of those things that just trips off the tongue, 'Yeah, I want to be a brilliant Dad (or Mum),' and everybody agrees: 'That's a great idea. What a wonderful plan.' Then you study the actions that you need to take, and being a brilliant parent is a massive task.

I'd like to tell you a story, and it's a personal story. I'm not making any apologies for this because at the end you'll see how you can apply this in many areas of your life as well. The reason I'm so excited about telling you this story is because I have seen the results week after week, month after month, year after year since I did one small thing in a brilliant way.

When my daughter was 6 years old, Valentine's Day was just around the corner. I remember thinking it might be a nice idea to get my daughter, Sarah, a Valentine's card. I did. It was the night before Valentine's Day. I was driving home, I was weary, I'd been working very hard and I pulled into a service station and went into the small shop. I remember standing looking at the depleted choice of cards that was available. There was one card that I felt was suitable. I took it home and wrote 'Happy Valentine's Day. Have a great one. I think you are wonderful', and tucked it under Sarah's pillow. The next morning she woke up. When she opened the card she looked at it, said 'Oh, that's nice.' She put the card on her shelf and went to school. Within a week the card had gone. You and I both know that it was a good job but the results, quite frankly, were poor.

Over the next year I started to get an understanding of what true brilliance was all about. I noticed Valentine's Day was coming up again (they conveniently put it on the same date every year) and I now had a real commitment to being a brilliant Dad. I started to think – what would a brilliant Dad do? He wouldn't be standing in a service station the night before looking for a card for his daughter; he would get a card in good time and he would make sure that card was important to her.

I started by talking at length to Sarah to get an understanding of what was important to her at that time. There were two main things. One was kittens and the other one was the pop group Steps. She loved the idea of getting a kitten and she loved listening to Steps and doing their dance moves. Next day I called the Steps marketing people and asked them if they had a Steps Valentine's card. The reply came, 'No I'm sorry we don't, but thank you very much for the idea.'

'OK,' I replied, 'do you have any new things available?'

'Yes we do. We've got some new merchandise which is going to be available for their tour which starts in the next couple of months.'

I was excited about the fact they were going on tour, but it transpired it was a sell-out. The kind chap in the Steps office told me that, on the following

Friday, four new dates were going to be announced, one in London, one in Manchester, one in Glasgow and one, locally to me, in Newcastle upon Tyne. Tickets would go on sale at 9 am!

I made a commitment to get tickets and formed a plan to acquire them. There are two ways you can buy tickets. Call the credit card hotline – take three telephones and call continuously, only to find out when you arrive at the concert that the tickets are miles from the stage! Or, the best way to get great tickets is to go and stand in the queue.

So that Friday morning I was up at 5 am, drove down to the Telewest Arena (now Metro Radio Arena) in Newcastle, walked around the corner and there in front of me, at 6 am were 500 kids all waiting to buy Steps tickets. Remember this is right at the beginning of February so it's really cold. Their Mums and Dads were standing around freezing but not the kids – they were dancing around a big 'ghetto blaster'.

I thought for about two seconds and made my mind up to be a kid. I jumped into the middle of the crowd. We were singing the songs, having a great time, and the hours passed very quickly. Eventually they opened the box office. I remember getting to the front of the queue and saying, 'I need two tickets which have a great view but I don't want them to be so close to the front that my daughter will be scared by the crowds.'

'Have a look at this,' said the lady in the box office as she produced a seating plan. She showed me two tickets which were on a slightly raised platform about 20 metres from the stage (you don't get tickets like that by calling the credit card hotline!). I took the tickets and gave myself a mental mark on the brilliance scale.

I had done **better than a good job**, but it still **wasn't brilliant,** *yet!*

The next thing I had to do was find the right type of Valentine's card. After I'd been to five or six shops, eventually I found a lovely card that had wonderfully cute kittens on the front. I wrote a little note inside saying, 'Sarah, would you like to go on a date with me on 21 May?' I popped the tickets inside and then realized there was one more thing I needed to do.

When we had been on holiday the year before, Sarah had fallen in love with a smell she found in a perfumery. It wasn't the nicest smell for me, it was what I would call an 'old man's' aftershave. Every day she used to spray this stuff on me as we walked past the local shops. She liked the smell. I looked around my local town to see if I could get it. Unfortunately I couldn't find it anywhere so I had to drive to Newcastle just to get a sample bottle and ask them to spray it into the card. I put the tickets in the envelope, sealed it up, wrote her name and address on and put it in the post. Why did I put it in the post and not underneath her pillow? Because kids love to get stuff in the post!

The morning of Valentine's Day arrived. Sarah came downstairs, ambled to the front door and then with a big huge smile on her face she picked up the post and said, 'Oh . . . two Valentine's cards for me!' As her Dad, I'm thinking who the other one was from! The first was from an elderly relative; she looked at it, put it on the shelf and that was it.

Then she opened the next one. As she opened it she immediately got an anchor. The anchor was, 'I can smell holidays.' A big smile appeared on her face. Then she took the card out of the envelope and she looked at the front and there was the picture of those cute kittens. Remember that kittens are number one on her important list at that time. She was going on and on, 'Oh, look at the kittens. Oh wow, they're so sweet.' In fact, she was so busy looking at the kittens that the tickets fell onto the floor. She opened the card and read the words out loud, 'Would you like to go on a date with me on 21 May?' Sarah looked around at me and said, 'Oh Dad, this must be from you. What are you up to? Come on Dad, what is it?'

I said, 'Sarah, have a look on the floor.' She looked down to the floor and she picked up the tickets. Her little mouth dropped open. She got so excited her legs started to go, her arms started to shake, her eyes became as wide as saucers. She was shouting 'Wow! Are we really going to see Steps?' 'Yes, we're really going to go, we're really going to go.'

That day, she took the tickets and the card to school and showed everybody. Luckily they came home. Then she made a countdown-to-Steps chart and started to learn all the dance moves and the songs (again!).

It got to the night of the concert. We drove down to Newcastle – she was really excited but also a little bit nervous. We walked in and started to move closer towards the front. Every time one of the security people stopped us they would check our tickets, point towards the front and say, 'Keep on walking, keep on walking.' We got closer and closer and closer to the front and Sarah's grip on my hand got tighter and tighter. When we got close to the stage, they pointed along a line of chairs and sure enough there they were, slightly raised at the front of a platform. We moved to the two centre seats – just for us! We watched an amazing show that evening – it was as if the whole concert was just for us. Sarah was jumping in the air and we had a night of dancing and singing.

We both had a brilliant time but the real true moment came for me when we were on the way home. We were in the car and Sarah turned to me and said, 'Daddy, today has been the best day of my life.' I'll always remember it because she said it with such sincerity, such belief that it truly was one of the greatest days of her life. It will stay with me for ever, but guess who else it stays with? Every time we drive past the arena, Sarah talks about the time when she went to see Steps and Dad gave her the card with the kittens on. She still has the card now years later and she's always telling her friends about this great evening, the card and the smell and the seats.

BRILL BIT

When you set a brilliant standard, you've got to step up continually. When you set a new standard for yourself and you understand why you want to be brilliant, it keeps you on the edge all the time. That's where the fun is, and that's where the enthusiasm for life comes from.

What's the message? Really simple: if being brilliant at something is important to you, make an honest judgement about where you are on the scale right now. Are you currently doing a poor job? Are you currently doing a good job? Or are you currently doing a fantastic job? Whichever one of those levels you find yourself on, the message is simple.

Step up!

You must step up to the next level. Once you decide to step up to that next level, do whatever it takes to achieve it – this is when you are going to reap the rewards. You don't just get good rewards, you don't get fantastic rewards, you get brilliant rewards.

Staying at the top

When planning a hotel stay these days millions of people visit the TripAdvisor website to see how others rate hotels in that location. In London there are well over a thousand hotels to choose from. Can you imagine how proud you would be if your hotel was in the top 10? Now think how it would feel to be in the top three. Now consider how it would feel if three of your properties were in the top three positions: one, two and three. This is the case for Red Carnation Hotels who have held the top positions for several years now and I am sure will continue to do so.

Yes, their hotels are beautiful, but so are lots of 'good' hotels. They have a very high staff-to-customer ratio, but so do lots of other 'fantastic' hotels. What makes them brilliant is the magical ways they find to make your stay amazing and memorable. I can't imagine staying in London and not choosing one of their hotels and I could fill pages with examples of their attention to detail and amazing service. However, this isn't a book on customer service, it's a book about brilliance, so I will give you just one example of when they absolutely shone.

My wife Christine is lactose intolerant. It's not a crazy eating fad, in fact it's very serious. If she should ingest cow's milk she becomes seriously ill and can be doubled up in pain for days. When we stayed in a Red Carnation Hotel, we mentioned at breakfast that Christine was lactose intolerant. They were great and very accommodating. But that's doing a good job.

Several weeks later we were back in London and we stayed in another Red Carnation Hotel. We were planning to go out for a meal, but that quickly changed when we got to our room. In our room there were two copies of the room service menu. The normal one and one in which the chef had taken the time to mark which items were dairy free and which could be adapted for those who had a lactose intolerance. We ate in. That's brilliance!

Red Carnation Hotels are now one of my clients. After a couple of nights staying at their hotels I made it a personal mission to get them as a customer. I could learn as much from them as they could from me. Perfect. I've also learned that if you want to be brilliant you should spend as much time as possible with other brilliant people and there's no better way than being a guest.

Taking action

Here is your next task. Take some time to think and reflect on what you would like to be brilliant at. If you are already good in an area, do you want to be better? If you have a passion for something, do you want to move up to brilliance? Start to think now. Once you get commitments, write them down. You may think of many things. A word of warning – the level of passion, enthusiasm and the amount of work that you are going to require to be brilliant will mean you need to narrow your list down to just two or three things at most. Do not ask 'How?' at this moment in time, and *do not* consider in any detail how you are going to do it. Further on in this book we'll be addressing all this. First, we are going to have a look at getting rid of what holds you back, creating a vision and putting together a plan on how you can truly step up to the level that you want to be on. It's the secret of how to be brilliant – it's about taking action now.

You may also be thinking, 'I'm going to do that. I'll start next week.' Remember, massive action equals massive results. So do it now!

Make a commitment to the **key areas** in your life where you want to be **brilliant right now**

Is it done? If it isn't, stop reading, go back and do it right now. This is important. This is going to change your life. Just reading will not make the difference to your life but taking action and writing things down will. This book is about taking action, so if you haven't done it – do it now.

So now you have decided on a maximum of three areas in which you want to be brilliant, give yourself a pat on the back. You are already a big part of the way there! Think for a moment about those areas. I guess that you are already thinking, 'Hmm … If I want to be brilliant in that area, why aren't I doing that now?' The reason is that there are things holding you back. The next chapter explores what those things are. In it you'll find out how to replace some of them with some more exciting powerful tools that will help you to achieve your vision in a tenth of the time that you thought would be possible.

BRILL BIT

Doing a good job isn't good enough. You will only get the rewards you deserve by doing a brilliant job, but brilliance doesn't happen by accident. You have to step up to the next level and focus on the areas where you want brilliance in your life right now.

Each of the stories in this chapter contains a message; every one of the people who we have studied so far uses many of the techniques covered, but they all have one thing in common. They have …

TEN YEARS ON

I'm reluctant to use a personal example in this update, but I have to share this one with you.

Going to the greatest show on earth

Since *How to Be Brilliant* was published there have been two more Olympic Games. And, of course, just when you think an Opening Ceremony can't get any better it does – twice.

Beijing went for size and London went for style. Both were brilliant, but I have to say London was best. Not just because it was our Olympic Opening Ceremony, and not just because of Danny Boyle's creative genius, but because … I was there.

After Sydney I got the bug for opening ceremonies, and when London was announced as the host city for 2012 I wrote in my diary under Friday 27th July 2012 'Opening Ceremony – no bookings today please – I will be there!'.

We applied for tickets (along with around three million other people) and guess what? We didn't get them. This is where you have to believe your own advice – there's always a way.

I made sure I was on every mailing list; I networked like crazy and asked everyone with ears if they knew a way to acquire Opening Ceremony tickets. There were a few dead ends but then something amazing happened.

About seven weeks before the opening date, I received a rather nondescript email from London 2012. They had been mailing almost every day with grand announcements of free events around the UK and ticket availability for events including the Switzerland vs South Korea football match. But this email was different.

London 2012 ticketing announced that more tickets would be released for events in the Olympic Stadium. They would go on sale at 11am the following morning. Apparently, when LOCOG had set up the TV cameras approximately 20 seats were freed up. The announcement was so low-key I was almost certain most people would miss it.

They didn't advertise the events they were selling but they listed a bunch of codes, and one of those codes was for the Opening Ceremony.

Quite promising.

So I spent most of the Thursday evening prior to the sale of tickets practising the process of buying tickets online. I noticed where I could shave a few seconds off the procedure and went through the buying process multiple times, much to the amusement of my family.

I was ready and confident that very few people would be aware of the type of tickets that were about to be released.

Then, disastrously, the next morning the headline news on Radio 2 was, 'The organisers of London 2012 are expecting a huge rush at 11am this morning when a handful of tickets are released for events in the Olympic Stadium. The tickets will be sold online on a first come, first served basis and they include the Men's 100 Metres Final and the Opening Ceremony.'

Could it get any worse?

Oh yes. It got a whole lot worse. TV stations ran the story. Newspapers ran the story. It was all over social media. By 10.30am most of Britain knew that in 30 minutes there was a chance they could get their hands on an elusive Olympic ticket.

However, here's where preparation meets opportunity. If I was going to secure my tickets I had to be better than good, better than fantastic – I had to be brilliant. And I was [smiling satisfied face].

At around 10.45am a friend of mine called me to share the news that most of Britain already knew. I thanked him and asked if he was going to attempt to buy tickets? He said he'd have given it a go but there was no real point as the people with the fastest internet connection were bound to get them first. This was a real slap in the face – living in rural Northumberland our internet speed could only be described as 'relaxed'.

By 10.50am I was in position. 'World Clock' was ticking in the corner of my screen. Credit card details were ready. Mobile phones and anything else that could get in the way were switched off. I closed my eyes and prepared with one last mental rehearsal.

At 10.59am and 58 seconds I hit refresh (I knew from the night before it took two seconds to refresh the page). And there they were. Again only listed as codes, but codes I knew by heart.

I clicked the Opening Ceremony number, entered two tickets, completed my personal details and hit the payment button. I had the long card number ready in my 'cut and paste' and knew all the other details by rote.

Boom, I hit return and crossed everything. I'd completed the whole process in less than 1 minute.

The next 35 seconds felt like an age as a wheel gently spun in the centre of the screen accompanied by the words 'please wait'. Then a totally understated message appeared. It simply informed me that I now had two tickets for the London 2012 Olympic Games Opening Ceremony.

A seven-year goal – achieved!

Perhaps you can see why, for me, London 2012 really was, and always will be, the greatest Opening Ceremony of all time.

5

BRILLIANT BELIEF SYSTEMS

What is it that drives you every day – and what is it that's holding you back? That's what we'll explore in this chapter. If there was nothing holding you back, you'd be achieving your dreams right now, right? You'd already be doing the things that you really want to be doing. So there must be some things that hold you back. The same kind of things that hold everybody back. They're known as limiting beliefs.

You are about to learn how to eliminate the limiting belief systems that are making it difficult for you to be all you can be. Instead, you'll replace them with something that is more exciting, more constructive. To get rid of unhelpful belief systems you need strong, compelling reasons for change, as a slight shift is not going to make the difference you need.

Imagine that you have a dodgy hard drive running programs in your head 24 hours a day, 7 days a week and this hard drive has been running for years and years. All the negative things you feel about yourself, everything you doubt about yourself, are all embedded in these programs that run continuously in your mind.

It's time to reformat the hard drive, and during this chapter you'll learn how. This part of the *How to Be Brilliant* process is essential. Without it, the programs (which you might not even be aware of) will drag you back, create obstacles and give you reasons why you shouldn't change. If you just take the hard drive and adjust one or two parts it's not going to be enough. I want you to take out the old, dodgy, hard drive, scratch it, smash it and destroy it so much that you'll want to get rid of it. You'll never want to use it again.

Then you'll want to replace it, immediately, with a brand new set of beliefs – empowering, exciting and driving beliefs. Some of the beliefs may be ones that you already have. I'm not suggesting you get rid of everything. You'll want to hold on to the parts of your life that are really fantastic. You'll want to build on those bits. However, I think it would be safe to guess that there are other parts of your life that you'd love to change right now!

I'm pretty sure that you will have a few questions in your head by now. What is a belief system anyway? Is it just something that we believe? How does it work?

Here's a simple example used by lots of trainers to explain belief systems. Imagine the table top is the belief system; it's something that you believe in, whatever it might be, it doesn't matter what it is – you believe it! The table top cannot stay there without the legs to support it. The legs are the evidence that supports the belief system.

Say you had a belief system of, 'I am an absolutely incredible, wonderful, beautiful person.' Could you find the evidence to support it? I'm sure you could (come on, think really, really hard!) . There might be times when you would catch a look in the mirror and think, 'Lookin' good'. You might get a compliment from somebody and hang on to it. You might do something for somebody and see

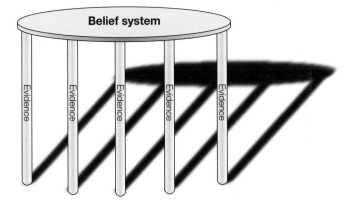

their appreciation and think, 'Wow. It was really great that I did that.' There is lots of evidence out there to support whatever belief system you might have.

You could also have a belief system that is, 'I'm an ugly pig and nobody likes me.' If you have that belief system, could you find a way to get the evidence to support it? Absolutely! Someone would make a comment about somebody else and you'd actually think they were talking about you. You glance in the mirror, when you're not looking your best, and you comment to yourself, 'Oh my God, that's what I look like!' You see other people who you believe look better than you and you say, 'Compared to them I'm hideous.' You get a pimple and you think everyone is looking at it. You can create any belief system and find evidence to support it.

Here is another example: remember September 11, 2001? It was a day that changed the world. Now go forwards to 21 September, 10 days later, and ask yourself this question as though you were there. Is today a good day to fly in America?

Some people have a belief system that says 'Yes, today is a great day to fly in America.' Other people have 'No, it is a terrible day to fly in America.' Which one is right? Well the truth is they are both right. And they will find different evidence to support their different viewpoints.

Take the belief system of the people who said 'No, it's not a good day to fly in America.' Why not? 'There are threats, delays. The newspapers say there are another thousand people out there who want to take over planes and do terrible things. It's a shocking time. That guy is a mad man and he'll do whatever it takes and the number-one target right now is America.' This is the evidence you can find when you have the belief system of 'No'. You'll always find the evidence that you need to support your table top. Do you think the newspapers made a difference to the available evidence 10 days after that event? Do you think news programmes, television, radio and gossip created enough evidence to support the fact that 21 September is not a good day to fly in America? Yes a huge amount of evidence was available to back up that point of view.

However, what if you had a belief system of, 'Yes, today is a great day to fly in America.' Could you find the evidence? Of course – what about the increased security? It's never been a safer time to fly. Amazing discounts and upgrades are available. It's a show of strength. There's never been a better time to fly in America.

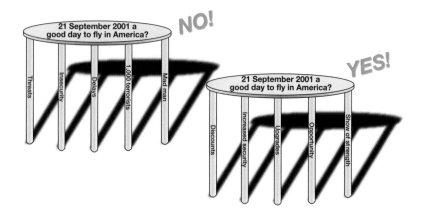

The reason I picked that date is because I had two phone calls, both from people in the United States on that day; a friend of mine who is English and a friend of mine who is American. The first conversation was with the Chairman of a huge organization for which we were organizing a conference. The American Chairman was supposed to be flying over to the UK to speak to his top sales people based throughout Europe. We had the whole event organized: big video screens, awesome PA system, amazing lights, superb venue, all the details were perfect. There was only one thing missing – the Chairman! And it was two days before the event. We were getting worried and then he called me to say, 'I won't be coming.'

'I can't believe this. Why not? Get on a plane and come over here now,' was my response.

'Well, I can't because it's not a very good time to fly, Michael.'

'No, it's a great time to fly. Get on a plane and come over here. Your top people from your organization want to meet you.'

'If they want to hear from me, can we do it by telephone?'

'Don't be crazy. You can't do it by telephone.'

'Can we do it by satellite? What if we paid for a satellite link, wouldn't that be cool?'

'No! You getting on a plane and coming over here to meet your European team – that would be cool.'

Unfortunately he never did get on that plane. He ended up doing a telephone link with his top guys. How do you think they felt? That their leader couldn't get on a plane? No surprise that he is no longer the Chairman of that company.

About five hours later I received another phone call from America. This time it was a friend of mine and she was giggling at the other end of the telephone. I asked, 'Where are you now?'

'I'm in America and you'll not believe what's happened, Michael. Three days ago I realized that I had a few weeks when I wasn't going to be doing much work and I had £1,000 saved. I made a decision to see how far I could travel on £1,000. Then the craziest thing happened this morning. I was in Washington, in Dulles Airport, I had slept on an airport bench overnight. I went to the desk of one of the big airlines this morning at 6 o'clock and I said to them, "Do you have any flights down to Florida?" I wanted to get as close to Orlando as possible. She said, "Yes, we normally do eight flights a day but we're down to two at the moment." I replied, "Great, could you have a look and see if there's any availability? But before you do, I'm going to make this easy for you. I only have $50, will you fly me to Orlando?" Her response was along the lines of, "We're really sorry, we do have some great discounts available at the moment but we can't fly you for $50."'

My friend said, 'No problem at all,' turned around and started to walk towards the American Airlines desk who were waving people over, had big smiles and were doing anything at all to get business at that point. She had only taken three steps when a voice from behind the original desk shouted 'Excuse me, Miss, if you come back over here we're going to see what we can do.'

Here's the best bit. My friend confidently walked up to them and said, 'You upset me, now you are going to have to upgrade me,' and sure enough they did! She flew Business Class from Washington to Orlando for $50 (including free champagne). When she arrived in Florida they were giving away free Disney tickets. Then she jumped aboard a free shuttle bus which took her to a decent hotel. She paid $20 a night to stay there! She went into Disney and when she walked through the gates they were so pleased to see her it was almost like, 'Quick, Mickey, put your head on. We have a guest!' There were no queues but the whole Disney atmosphere was there. It was incredible.

She finished her conversation by saying, 'Michael, there's never been a better time to fly in America.'

BRILL BIT

Two people both with totally different belief systems. Which one was right? They were both right! I would never say that a belief system is wrong but, what I would say is, one of those people had an empowering belief system; the other had a disempowering belief system. You know exactly which one had the empowering belief system and which one had the disempowering belief system. They both found the evidence that was necessary to support whatever they believed at that particular time.

So what is *your* belief system?

Take a look at what this really means in very simple terms.

If you have a **belief system**, you **will** find the evidence to support it

Go back to the areas where you said you wanted to be brilliant. Take the first one and then write down all the things that are holding you back from achieving brilliance in that area of your life. Yes *all* the things that are holding you back. Everything! Write down all the limiting beliefs you believe you can control and the ones that you believe you can't. Write everything down.

If you are reading this right now and thinking, 'I can only think of one or two things that are holding me back' then that's rubbish. You're just not thinking hard enough yet. Here are some clues:

Time	Debts
Money	Knowledge
Location	Qualifications
My boss	Being a woman
My partner	Being a man
Disability	Lack of transport
Being too fat	Fear of failure
Being too thin	Worrying about others
Lack of confidence	Illness
Lack of trust	Children
No support	Race
Laziness	Religion

There are so many things. If you're completely honest about *all* the things that hold you back, you'll be able to write quite a long list. Don't stop writing; just keep on going, keep that momentum, keep your physiology strong and just remember not to hold back. This is for you, so write everything down, everything you can.

The only reason you should be continuing to read this chapter is because you have a full and complete list of things that are holding you back. You are probably thinking, 'Wait a minute. I thought this was going to be a positive, motivational book. I have written down all this stuff and it would depress me if I focused on it.' If so, good – that's exactly how it should feel. The good news is you are going to get rid of it.

The only way of moving forward is to be aware of the things that are holding you back. This awareness is going to make such a difference as you move to the next stage of the process. Now I'm going to assume you've completed your list.

If you read your list, my guess is that as you look at some of the things that you wrote down you're thinking 'That's crazy. Why do I let that happen?' You could choose right now never to think about that again or do those crazy things. You could choose right now to change your belief system instantly and once you decide to change, you need never go back. You could do that right now with several things that are on the list, I am sure. Find them and tick them off your list. They are the easy ones. That was all you needed to do – to make a decision and know you will stick with it by using true will.

Then there are others. When you look at them, you say, 'Wow, that's big stuff!' They are the real issues. They are the big ones. So underline or put a star, draw circles around or do something that emphasizes they are key problems – big challenges.

Did you do it? I hope so. If you did, you should now have a real understanding of what is holding you back from brilliance. Now look at those items and ask yourself, 'How would it feel if I could get rid of those things from my life – for ever?'

Already there's a part of your brain that is trying to be heard. It's a sneaky part of your mind – the part that introduces self-doubt. And that part of your brain is probably saying, 'I can never change those things. It's just what life's like. Other people will think I'm crazy if I do that. Who on earth do I think I am?'

Just tell that part of your brain to shut up for a moment. It can have its time later when you have your new belief system in place!

The final part is very easy. When you look at your list, there will be one huge item. And when you look at that item, you think: 'Wow! That is just so big that I cannot go over it. It's so wide I can't go around it. It's so huge I can't go under it.' I call it the 'Rock'. It's the number-one thing that holds you back. You could ignore it or decide you'll work on it later after you've tackled some of the smaller limiting beliefs. Or you could be brave and do what thousands of others have done whilst reading this book, and make a decision to get rid of it right now using …

TEN YEARS ON

9/11 is an event that will be remembered forever. However, I was in two minds whether to remove the story of the two travellers who made such different choices after that September day in 2001. Was there another example that is more recent or more relevant? I don't think so. It was such a massive event in world history that I am confident those two people and their differing beliefs are something that everyone can still relate to.

The global financial crisis has probably affected more people, as some people/organizations went into free fall. Newspapers told us we were reliving the Wall Street Crash of 1929. My experience was varied, but most people I came into contact with had the same belief system – they just worked harder. They understood they had to 'add value' and just got on with it. They understood that pay rises were out of the question for a few years and that spending more than you earned was history. It's a shame various governments didn't understand that basic economic principle!

I don't know what they will be or when they will happen, but I do know (if the last 10 years are anything to go by) that there will be life-changing events across the world in the next few years.

It's unlikely that you will ever have a choice as to whether they will happen, but you will always have choice over how you react to them.

6

BRILLIANT
ROCK-BUSTING

want you to identify what you truly believe is the Rock. Do it right now and mark it.

Guess which one you are going to start with? That's right, you're going to start with the big one, the Rock. It's no good fooling around just getting rid of little pebbles when you can go and do some big rock-busting!

You may have a Rock that somebody else would look at and say:

★ What do you mean you are too young?

★ What do you mean you are too old?

★ What do you mean you haven't got the qualifications?

★ What do you mean that you aren't fit enough?

★ What do you mean that your family is holding you back?

★ What do you mean that you don't have enough belief in what you do and fear failure?

★ What do you mean you haven't got enough resources?

★ What do you mean you haven't got enough money?

★ Why on earth do you think *you* lack confidence?'

They can't understand why you have that Rock and you probably can't understand theirs either. The only reason why it is real for you is because you have created the evidence to support it.

Here is what you are going to do. Just for fun, use your imagination. *You* are going to be playful and see if *you* can create an affirmation; some words that, when used, would be the absolute total antithesis of what the Rock is, or what it means to you. Doing this won't get rid of it; this is just a starting point.

I'm really into practical methods and I love simple tools. I don't believe that if you just chant something for long enough that you are going to get rid of a problem. That's like going back to, 'No weeds, no weeds'. You don't want to simply stand and say, 'No Rock, no Rock.' That isn't going to get rid of your Rock.

Changing your language

I want you to give your brain a whack and create a different way of looking at the problem. The way you're going to do this is you're going to change the way that you think about this particular challenge. You're going to start by messing up the hard drive I mentioned at the start of the last chapter. You're going to destroy (or reformat if you're into recycling) that old hard drive and start to create some new data that is the absolute opposite of where you were before. To do this it's best to start with something simple, like self-talk. This is the internal chatter you play in your mind when you're faced with the Rock. Here are a few examples:

Lack of confidence

'I'm not a confident person.' Or 'I'm shy.' You know when people say that then automatically they have that as a Rock. It makes perfect sense: if you *say* you're 'not confident', if you *say* 'shy', if you *act* shy and retiring, what type of results are you going to get? You'll create a belief system and find the evidence you need to back up your lack of confidence.

What if, instead, you created a new affirmation, a new belief system, one that is empowering? Something like, 'I have all the confidence that I need now.' You'll start to see and feel yourself being confident. Can you visualize yourself being outgoing, meeting people, smiling? So rather than saying 'Oh, I'm not very confident,' start to tell yourself, 'I have all the confidence that I need now.'

Not enough time

'Oh, I haven't got the time'; 'There are not enough hours in the day'; 'You don't know everything I have to do.'

Here's a secret … We all have the same amount of time. Some people just seem to manage it better than others. So what about instead of 'I haven't got the time' you say, 'I can find the time for everything that's important to me now.' Or simply: 'I can find the time.' Do you see how the choice of words is so important? Go on, say it out loud, 'I can find the time for everything that is important to me now.' Great affirmation!

'I'm too old' or 'I'm too young'

Depending on how old you are, I'll give you a few different examples. What if your belief system was, 'I'm too old'. Could you instead say, 'My experience and wisdom puts me ahead of the game'? That is a great place to be, 'ahead of the game'. What if your belief system is, 'I'm too young' and you worry about not having enough experience? Could you instead say 'My innocence, my passion, my vibrancy will help me to achieve anything I put my mind to'? Isn't that more empowering than 'I'm too young'?

'I haven't got enough money'

Have you heard anybody say that one? That might be your Rock. It's a common one. I know that it's a massive issue right now and one that needs more than a few affirmations. However, what if you were to start by saying instead, 'All that I need is within me now!' Think about the earth as an abundant place. See the earth as an abundant place and feel the abundance coming towards you. Visualize your resources, the money or whatever it needs to be, coming towards you and tell yourself, 'All that I need is within me now.' It is the antithesis of the disempowering, 'I haven't got enough money'! If you still need some convincing then start asking yourself a different question. 'How can I find a way to have this?' You'll be amazed at what your brilliant brain thinks of.

'I'm lazy' or 'I procrastinate'

Another classic, which I hear a lot of people saying is: 'I'm just lazy', 'I'm a procrastinator', 'I *should* do more', 'I should do this. I should do that.' I heard this from Tony Robbins, the life coach we met earlier, about 'should'. 'When people say I *should* do this, I *should* do that, you know what's going to happen? They're going to *should* all over themselves! You have to make it a must.' Brilliant!

So instead of saying 'I'm lazy', you could say, 'I have the enthusiasm, drive and energy to achieve anything that I put my mind to. I make it a must!'

> **BRILL BIT**
>
> As you start to use different language, particularly strong affirmations, you begin to take different actions. This isn't 'airy fairy' stuff; it isn't flowery language for the sake of it. This is you starting to reprogramme your nervous system, reprogramming the way that you think by changing your choice of words. And best of all you will get immediate, noticeably different results.

Words are a great foundation but on their own they are not enough. At the end of the day, it all comes down to the actions that you take. Actions are the most important thing. As you play with the words, don't just say them in your head – say them out loud. The physiology of speaking out loud will make this stick faster. When you have played with those words, looked at the right adjectives, listened for the right tonality – when you have really thought about it, say it out loud again and again so it becomes part of you.

You want this new empowering language to be something that you will say on a frequent basis. So even if that old Rock starts to sneak back later after you have eliminated it – if you get a small seed of doubt – you can come right back with your new affirmation.

Taking massive action

Here are two more techniques for eliminating the Rock and all those other limiting beliefs you listed before. The reason you start with the Rock is that once you have removed it, you can get rid of your other limiting beliefs fairly easily. Time to break it down and destroy your limiting belief systems one by one. Some of them are going to be blasted out of the water, others are going to take a bit more effort.

The first technique you will use is very practical. The second one is much more intuitive and involves you using a part of your brain that you may not access too often.

Circles of Influence versus Circles of Concern

The first idea is called 'Circles of Influence versus Circles of Concern', and it's adapted from a concept that was used by Dr Stephen Covey. This is a method that relies on you sitting down, putting pen to paper, developing structured solutions and looking at clear strategies.

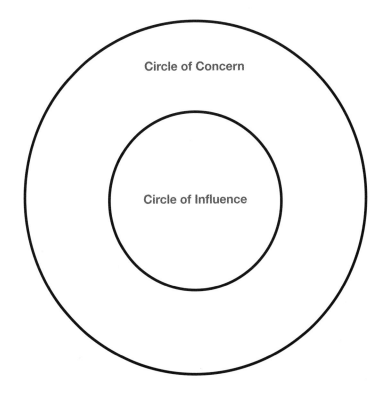

Circle of Concern

Circle of Influence

Look at the diagram; you'll notice that there are two circles. The big circle is the Circle of Concern. This circle is the one that holds all the problems, all the concerns, all the worries, all the things that are holding you back. It truly is a Circle of Concern. The great thing about the Circle of Concern, even though it is there and it is very real, is you don't have to do anything about it! All you have to do is be *concerned* about those things; you don't have to take any actions. You can moan and groan about it all day, it doesn't matter. You don't have to take any actions!

I'm sure you'll know some people who love to spend all their time in their Circle of Concern. In fact, the more time they can spend in their Circle of Concern the better; for them it's a great place to be because it's comfortable. Also, people give you sympathy and attention when you are in your Circle of Concern – especially if you talk about your concerns a lot. They understand you have problems. They feel sorry for you. And that feels so good you find yourself hanging on to that problem. The challenge is you won't be able to move on to the next level and achieve brilliance if you do that. So it's time to refocus your attention now.

Here's what you do. Use the Circle of Concern and fill in as many concerns around your Rock as you can. List all the things that are holding you back: what other people say, how you feel about it, the results, the actions, the problems, everything. Put it all in to the Circle of Concern. Go on, see if you can fill the whole of that big fat circle with concerns, even if it looks like a mad ramble on the paper, just keep writing all the things, all the concerns, write as many as you can. Do the exercise right now.

Now you have a **circle full of concerns**,

what are you going to do about it?

You could continue to focus on the Circle of Concern, but if you do, your smaller circle, the Circle of Influence, would start to get smaller and smaller. Eventually the Circle of Influence (what you can truly do about your situation) will shrink so small that it really would make you feel, 'There is nothing I can do.'

Before it has a chance to do that, let's change your focus. Just think of one thing, one key thing, to put into your Circle of Influence. A specific idea, that when you write it *and take action*, it will make some difference to eliminating the Rock. It doesn't matter how small it is, it doesn't matter how spectacular it is, just think of one idea and write it in your Circle of Influence. One idea, one thing that you can do in your Circle of Influence that will make a difference. Do it now.

If you wrote, 'Change my attitude', 'Find some time' or something vague like that, then as your coach I'm going to give you a 'Must try harder'! Get specific about what you're going to do. If you have 'Lack of confidence' as your Rock and you wrote, 'Try to be more confident', then not a great deal will change. If you want to be brilliant at change, you need to take clear and specific actions. Something like 'Read five books on building confidence.' Then find five ideas from each book that you can apply, measure the difference they make and then focus on mastering those ideas.

Or if you had something about not having enough qualifications and you wrote, 'Get some qualifications', then again this is too vague. Instead go for something like, 'Prepare a list of all the qualifications I need by asking key influencers what they think I should have. Get a list of all the courses available in my area and find the one that is most suited to me. Meet with the tutors and decide if this is the right route for me to take.' Can you see how much more powerful that type of action is?

Once you have thought of one thing, you might be able to think of two things or even three. At that point, stop. You only ever have a maximum of three actions in your Circle of Influence.

When you start to crack that Rock you'll start to make smaller stones, those stones become tiny stones, those tiny stones become pebbles, and those pebbles become sand. Sand can be brushed away.

The three rules to remember when completing your Circles of Influence and Circles of Concern are:

1 Always acknowledge the concerns before you move on to what you can influence.

2 Only have three positive actions in your Circle of Influence, never more.

3 Always make the actions entered in the Circle of Influence clear, positive and specific.

Brilliant! I don't know if you have realized, but you've already started on your plan. Take a look at where you were a few chapters ago. Before Chapter 3 you were probably unaware of what was really important, and what you wanted to be brilliant at. Remember, you made a decision about what you wanted to be brilliant at and you recognized there are things that are holding you back. Very few people ever go through this process; very few people have really thought about what was holding them back. Then you took an opportunity to identify those different challenges; I know there are many, many different challenges but I asked you to get focused. You then identified the ones that were causing the biggest problems of all.

From there, in this chapter, you moved to the next stage and acknowledged the big one, the Rock; the one that, if you could get rid of it, would make such a huge difference. Then you attacked the challenge by exploring a different way to look at the situation. You started to create a new belief system and focused on your self-talk. You didn't have much evidence but all you had to do was to choose new words and create a new affirmation.

The next stage was amazing because you really focused, using your Circle of Influence and Circle of Concern. You decided that you don't want to spend another moment focusing on those concerns because your new focus is now going to be on those one, two or three things in your Circle of Influence, the ones that are going to make a difference.

As you do this, you'll start to see your Circle of Influence getting bigger, and the bigger it gets, the stronger it becomes. And the more you'll feel yourself becoming confident about tackling the challenges.

I guarantee that any challenges you have will become less and less significant in your life and the new belief system, the new one that you are creating right now, will start to take over.

I want to give you more tools further on in this book for creating a vision, for finding people who can help you, to look at ways you can raise your game, to understand how you can change your physiology, and how you can mentally rehearse. But take a moment to reflect, as this is an important moment – you've started the process of being brilliant now!

BRILL BIT

Understanding that brilliance doesn't happen by accident and that brilliant people have a range of tools to move forward in a number of different ways is a fundamental part of the process. Brilliance is within your grasp!

Brilliant intuition: the Mastermind Group

This is a much deeper, more intuitive way to tackle a particular problem and it's called using your 'Mastermind Group'. Your intuition is the most incredible, amazing thing that you have. The answer to many problems and challenges and the solution to so many questions are right there in your intuition, right now.

Would you like to know how to develop **your intuition** so that you can **tap into it** whenever you need to?

I remember reading one of the very first personal development books ever written; it's called, *Think and Grow Rich* by Napoleon Hill. Napoleon Hill was absolutely inspirational. He found the most successful people on the planet and studied what it was that made them so effective. He interviewed 500 people over a period of 20 years. He met with Presidents, he consulted the leaders of industry, interrogated leaders of communities, and found that they all had certain things in common. The characteristics we explored in Chapter 2 were all there but also many of these successful people had a group of people whom Hill referred to as a 'Mastermind Group'. This was a group of people whom they could sit down with and who would give them great advice. They were often people of great distinction and intellect or those with many years of experience.

But what about you? You don't have access to these amazing people to give you advice, do you? Well you may not have them with you physically but you could have them with you mentally. As well as the face-to-face advice the Mastermind Group can give, highly successful people also know how to tap into their intuition and ask, 'What would this member of my Mastermind Group do?' That way they can have access to great minds 24/7.

Here's how to create and tap into the knowledge of your own Mastermind Group.

Start by making a list of the people who you admire and whose advice you would trust. Close your eyes, relax and create a brilliant meeting area in your imagination. It could be around a camp fire for a pow-wow or a boardroom for a power meeting. It's up to you.

Now imagine where you would sit each member of your Mastermind Group. Introduce them to one another – it's fun! Finally, with your eyes closed, and in a relaxed state, imagine having a conversation with your new (mental) mentors.

You can ask your Mastermind Group about issues you face, work or personal challenges, what you might do next, or how to deal with a tricky situation. It's your agenda and everyone is there to help you. Each member of your Mastermind Group will give you their take and offer pearls of wisdom. When you have your answers, open your eyes and take action!

I was once teaching a group of very serious business leaders this technique and after testing it one said to me, 'Michael, I have a concern. I can see the group, I've introduced them to each other and I've given them a challenge to consider. However, when they feed back it's like I'm doing all the thinking rather than them just talking.' 'Yes! That's exactly how it should feel,' I told him, 'It's when you have voices in your head that you aren't controlling you need to be concerned!'

This tool is simply there to help you to dig deep into your intuition and find a way of clarifying what you probably already knew but needed some help with.

So now you know how to surround yourself with amazing people whom you can ask for advice, simply by closing your eyes and using your imagination. But what about the real thing? Aren't there living, breathing, amazing people on the planet who you'd love to ask for advice and hear what they've got to say for real? Of course there are!

Did you know there is a superb technique that you can use if you ever need advice from somebody that will make them want to help you? And it's just a few magic words. Learning and using these words will make a big difference in your life. The magic words are ...

TEN YEARS ON

Probably the biggest change in the last 10 years is the amount of 'rocks' that appear to be outside of our control.

Many people feel that things have 'happened to them', without their actions or behaviours having had any impact on their current situation. I can't argue with that. However, what's more important than ever is to have the belief that there is always something you can do. No matter how small, there's always something. That's the power of the Circle of Influence.

When I present How to Be Brilliant as a workshop, I challenge the audience with a bold statement. It goes along the lines of, 'We've been teaching this programme for 16 years to half-a-million people around the world and I have yet to meet someone who couldn't find anything to put in their Circle of Influence.'

Of course, once I lay down this gauntlet the nay-sayers are all over it – determined to show me that their 'rock' is unique, worse than anyone else's and there really is *nothing* they can do about it.

Here are two of the more unique ones I've heard in the last 10 years:

One of the more unusual ones was: 'I have to look after my dog'. Seriously, this person believed they couldn't go for a promotion, change jobs or take on any more responsibility because it would mean they'd have less time and may neglect their dog.

They had never done a Google search on 'Ideas to help busy people look after pets'. They hadn't talked to their boss. Their boss who, by the way, was on the same course, lived on their own, commuted over an hour (each way) from their office and had two dogs.

A more serious rock, which was shared by a participant in tears, was this: 'My friend's marriage broke down because she became more successful than her partner and I don't want that to happen to me.'

Wow, that's a rock.

The good news with this one was we were working with a small group of mid-level managers who really cared about each other.

The best and simplest idea was to get her partner involved with her success plan. In other words, let HIM think he was a big part of the accomplishment. Simple psychology.

There are hundreds of rocks and thousands of permutations, and in over 16 years working with half-a-million people I have yet to be beaten. There's ALWAYS *something* you can do. Even if you have nothing else, you still have *choice* over your reaction to the situation.

7

I NEED YOUR HELP

As you become more successful and begin to achieve your goals then life becomes easier, right? Actually, no. The truth is that in most cases life actually becomes increasing complicated. And with your new-found success comes increased responsibility, pressure and numerous time-sapping activities.

Brilliant people know this, they plan for it and most importantly surround themselves with people who can help them to reach their next level. At the same time they leave behind much of the complexity that holds others back.

Even if you think you do not have that level of success yet, it's worth learning and creating habits now that will enable you to keep moving to ever higher levels of brilliance in the future.

Here's how …

1 Get your mind-set right

You can't, shouldn't and won't be able to do it all on your own. Get that into your head right now before you read another word. I don't care how independent you want to be, how much you think you can do, or how bad you may feel about asking other people for help, you must accept this in order to be brilliant at anything. You'll achieve brilliance faster, more easily and (in most cases) more effectively if you involve others.

Now we've established that, and you've accepted it, you can move on.

2 Learn the magic words

Four words. Yes, just four, simple, one-syllable words, when put in the right order and delivered in the right way, will transform your life forever.

That's it. So humble, but don't be fooled by the simplicity of these words. Use them correctly and they'll change your life.

This whole chapter is about asking for help and I'll cover it more in the coming pages. This first part is specifically about *how* to ask for help. And in my experience there is no better way than to use the magic words. It's as if the human brain is pre-programmed with a switch that when it hears those words in that exact order it moves into 'How can I help?' mode.

The words are …

I've tested multiple versions of the magic words and none has achieved anything like the results of 'I need your help'. And as crazy as it seems I want you to practise saying those words, out loud, right now.

If you're reading this in a public place then I'll allow you a timeout until you feel comfortable, but I do want you to say them in different ways, using different tones and inflection.

Here's a quick example of how not to and how to ask for help. First, here's how *not* to ask for an introduction:

TOM *'Hi Sue, you know that contact of yours in the city? Would you introduce me to him?'*

SUE *'I'll see what I can do. What's it about?'*

And here's how to ask for an introduction using the magic words:

TOM *'Hi Sue. I need your help.'*

SUE *'Sure Tom, what is it?'*

TOM *'I need an introduction to your friend in the city.'*

I know it's only a subtle difference but so is the difference between fantastic and brilliant.

Learn these words, practise saying them and put them to the test.

3 Ask the right people

Here's a paraphrased quote from Charlie 'Tremendous' Jones, who all his life was on a mission to do better, be better and find ways to help others do the same:

> 'You will be in five years the sum total of the books you read and the people you are around.'

Well done with your book choice by the way! When I coach people I frequently find myself challenging my clients about the company they keep. They surround themselves with uninspiring people who are happy with below average results and then they wonder why they aren't living fulfilling lives.

Worse than that, they then ask the same uninspiring people for advice!

If you are going to have brilliance as your benchmark then you must find some inspirational people to help you. They don't have to be famous, rich or world leaders. Just the ones who've been there, done it and proudly wear the T-shirt.

4 Prepare yourself

Use the advice from this book to mentally prepare yourself for success. It's much easier to take the middle ground, make no decisions (to avoid making the wrong one) and procrastinate rather than taking action. It's time to be different and get yourself organised, motivated and ready for action. This is an essential step in preparing to engage others in your plan to be brilliant!

5 Have a plan

It's difficult to ask for help if you don't know what you're asking help for. So take a little time to work out what you need help with. Here are a few clues:

★ introductions
★ specialist knowledge
★ time

* practical advice
* how to's
* mistakes to avoid
* faster ways of achieving
* to borrow resources
* to review what you've done
* a step up the ladder.

Having a plan will accelerate your success rate significantly, it's time well invested, so get it done – now!

6 Know who to ask and when to ask them

Assuming you've completed your plan, then the next stage is to develop your relationships with the people who can help you and, ultimately, to get them involved.

You can do this by creating a 'Farm List'. Farmers don't use all of their land all of the time. Some fields are being planted while others are harvested, some are left to go fallow while others have livestock. Farmers are patient. Harvest too soon and you won't reap the rewards of the crop. However, if you leave it too late to plant you'll miss your moment and be left with barren fields.

Once you've decided on your plan, make time to decide who can help you and when you will need them. You'll have three types of people on your list:

* Ripe and ready. Some people will be ready and in place right now. They're just waiting to be asked. Don't leave it too long. If your intuition says these people are in place and could be happy to help you, then go for it.

* Planting the seeds. Others you may not feel close enough to, or have a strong enough relationship with. It doesn't mean you're not going to bother with them. Write a list of these people; think what you can do to nurture the relationship. Just like the farmers and their crops, you know you have to invest time and care in the early stages without taking anything out. Patience is the key.

* Already harvested. With a few you may feel like you have already taken enough or even too much from the relationship. These people, just like the fields, need to be tendered, nurtured and, in some instances, left to go fallow before you start the seeding and growing process again. Don't over-harvest the crop.

New land

Once you've decided who can help you and when you are going to ask them, you may find that you have a few gaps. If that's the case then you need to find completely different people who can help you. My advice is to meet as many people as possible and do something for them. Helping others first is the secret fertilizer that will accelerate the process so that ultimately, they will be ready to help you.

The good news is that, unlike the farmer, you don't have to wait for nature – you can do this whole process in weeks, or even days.

7 Be generous, honest and faithful

Asking for help works – especially if you take the time to learn and use this system. However, it won't work unless you are generous, honest and faithful. Here's why:

★ **Be generous.** So how are you when it comes to giving help? If you think this system is all about what you can get, then think again. You'll be asked for help on this journey too. What will you say?

★ **Be honest.** When you are asking people to help you they'll appreciate your honesty. Be absolutely clear about what you want them to do. If you are working on your Farm List, ensure you are building the right relationships for the right reasons. *Never* build a relationship to manipulate someone.

★ **Be faithful.** When you are given an introduction or some advice, see it through. Go back to the person who helped you and let them know how things are going. Never miss an opportunity to do something for them. Close the loop.

Taking action

So that's it. Simple? Yes. Effective? Extremely! So would you like to know how you can make it even better?

Over the years I've met many people who have read this book. They like the idea of the four magic words – 'I need your help'. They can see how it could work. Their challenge? A lack of action.

Now if that's you, and there's no hiding here because you'll only be kidding yourself, then may I suggest you just test out this 'I need your help' idea once – yes just once – in the next 24 hours? It might be asking the kids to empty the dishwasher, finding a colleague who could give you a hand or, if you've written your plan, approaching the first person on your Farm List. By taking action, you start to create momentum and quickly this leads to opportunities. Opportunities for you to grasp on your journey to being brilliant.

If you know more than five people then you are in luck and I'm prepared to make a bet with you. I'll wager £5 right now that you can't ask all five people for help using the method I've just shared with you and get five outright no's.

This means that you **must** and **will** get some help **in your goal** towards achieving brilliance!

Find a mentor (or two)

Mentors are slightly different from the people on your 'I need your help' list. You'll be looking to build a longer-term relationship with them.

One of the keys to how to be brilliant is to find mentors who will push you, advise you, coach and encourage you. Mentors are better than you! Asking a mate if he or she will be a mentor in most cases won't help. Asking a person who is the best you know in your field, sport, hobby, interest, industry etc. is a far more effective way of getting results.

Meet with your mentors regularly and keep them informed of your progress. If you have chosen well, your mentors will be very successful and probably very busy. Don't let them down. Your mentors will also be able to introduce you to people who will make things happen faster and bigger. Treat your mentors with respect. One day you will be able to do something for them. When this day comes, take this opportunity and make it happen quickly.

BRILL BIT

The first time you meet your mentor formally, take them a gift. Make it personal and imaginative. If possible, write a message on it; if not, attach a card with a message neatly written inside. Your mentor will be grateful, but more importantly they will show others and the contacts will flow.

Developing your Mastermind Group

As I said at the end of the last chapter you can use your imagination to create a powerful Mastermind Group. That's when your intuition is going to come into place to use the power of visualization. Visualization is amazing because there are no limits to it. Which is the biggest nation in the world? Not China, not

America. The biggest nation in the world is your imagination. Corny, I know, but you'll be using it!

Now is a good time to consider who you want to have in your Mastermind Group. If you could have Winston Churchill as an advisor or mentor, would you accept him? What about Richard Branson or Billy Connolly? Using your imagination, you can. Your Mastermind Group can be people from history. They can be people whom you admire. They can be people whom you have read about. Just start and imagine each of those places being filled with a person who can give you great advice.

If you haven't done this yet, stop reading for a moment and take a few minutes to create your Mastermind Group. Then give it a go and mentally have a conversation with those people and ask them for advice. Let your mind go for it here – really explore the views of your Mastermind Group.

How did you find that? Sometimes when I have done this with people I have spent a lot of time getting them very relaxed, going through the process and at the end of it they have said, 'Well it was OK, but ... I was really surprised by the people I had in my head – Gandhi, Billy Connolly, the Queen and a friend of mine from school!' My advice is just to go with it. Your Mastermind Group comes together for a reason and the reason is to help you tap in to that brilliant intuition of yours.

Here's something interesting about intuition – your intuition will always be right. It will always be right even if you think it's wrong. Sometimes your intuition will tell you something, you'll get a message but you won't quite understand *why* you've got that particular message. What tends to happen is, suddenly, at a later point, something occurs and your intuitive thought makes sense. You'll have that eureka moment when you just know, 'That's what it meant! Now I get it!'

BRILL BIT

Visualization is a wonderful way to develop your intuition. Intuition is a wonderful way to find solutions to different challenges at different levels. The secret to this technique is to play full out with it and really let your mind go.

Really letting your mind go is important. Imagine if you sit down and say 'OK, I'm going to close my eyes now and I'm going to picture Richard Branson.' In your visualization you then say, 'Hi Richard, how do I make a lot of money?' Branson replies 'Work hard!' You open your eyes and say, 'That didn't work.' If you think like that, guess what's going to happen? You're not going to get the results that you want.

But if you decide, 'I'm going to go for this' and open your mind to possibility thinking then you will love the results. I'm going to ask lots of questions and go with the flow. You will get amazing responses.

You could choose Richard Branson or Alan Sugar for business advice. You could have a top agony aunt for relationship advice! Or you may choose somebody from your past who has always been there and given you great counsel before. When you sit down with those people in your imagination and really let yourself go and get a feel for what it is they're saying then you'll be astounded by what you think of.

Imagine getting some of the top thinkers in the world to help you to work on eliminating your Rock. Make this a must. Once you've got your advice and taken massive action I'm sure you know what's going to happen to that Rock.

You're taking **dynamite** to it! There's no longer a little crack there; you're starting to **blow it to pieces**

It doesn't have to stop there, not just with the Rock. You can use your intuition for so many different areas of your life. So develop it, learn from it, grow with it, but above all, trust it.

Once the Rocks begin to disappear and the confidence grows, I have often found people believe they are liberated. Then as quickly as they found their success, they begin to lose it. Their life seems to go out of balance and they find that, even with their success, they haven't found happiness.

Don't worry, this won't happen to you. You will be successful, brilliant and happy. How do I know? Because you'll have …

TEN YEARS ON

Looking at the past 10 years, I don't have many regrets other than I wish I'd asked more people for help. I've had two coaches and half-a-dozen mentors during that time, and the knowledge they have shared has done so much for my personal development I can't help thinking, what if I'd asked for more help?

However, I have also had the pleasure of helping many others during that time and received massive personal growth because of that.

Build and use your own 'Farm list'

Since *How to Be Brilliant* was first published we've had hundreds of emails from readers asking for help. While we (the Michael Heppell Ltd team) do our best to offer support and advice, I think it's better to use your own personal 'Farm List' (step 6) than ask someone whom you don't know.

Maybe in the original book I didn't make this clear enough. That section is updated now, with much more information on developing and using your Farm List.

Plus, it's never been easier to connect or reconnect with people who want to be connected with. Business connections through the likes of LinkedIn are very powerful. Facebook is a great way to develop personal connections, and a much better use of your online time than 'liking' yet another 'poor me' status or commenting on your friend's fab 'selfie'.

Farm Lists are a brilliant way to find someone to help you with a challenge. Don't wait for 10 years and wish you'd asked for help. Find the right people. Ask the right people. And do it now.

BRILLIANT VALUES

Values are the nervous system of a brilliant life. They connect everything to everything. Put simply, values are right up there with oxygen!

Sir John Templeton became one of the most successful investors of all time and a billionaire in the process. His deep-rooted values meant he would not be swayed to move from his core beliefs. He would save and invest 50 per cent of his income (a value and habit he developed before he became a professional investor) and he would give millions of dollars to worthy causes every year as well as supporting numerous individuals and projects. He has written many books about the significance of a spiritual life and the importance of giving.

Bernard Madoff also acquired massive wealth. He did so by running one of the biggest financial scams in history. His values were based on greed and a belief that he could keep taking money (even from an employee benefit plan) without being caught. Eventually his own sons reported him to the authorities and he was sentenced to 150 years in prison. He too would not be swayed from his values.

What type of wealthy person would you like to be? In the case of the people mentioned, money simply magnified their values.

As you read this chapter, there may be times when you think, 'Where is he going here?' or 'What do you want me to achieve from this?' At this point it is important that you stick with the chapter. When I ask you to do an exercise, complete it thoroughly before moving on to the next stage. This is an important foundation on which you'll build your brilliant future.

I want to start off by asking you an important question:

What is your question?

What is your Life Question? What question do you find yourself asking more than any other throughout the day?

Right now you may be thinking, 'I don't have a question. There's really nothing I can think of that I ask myself repeatedly', or even 'I don't know what you mean!'

That's OK. Let me give you some examples of other people's Life Questions – then you may start to get an idea of what it is that you might be asking yourself, maybe without realizing it. It's important that you don't judge any questions; I just want you to be aware of whatever it is that's in your head.

Here's a list of some of the Life Questions that other people ask themselves:

★ How can I be part of this?

★ What can I do to make this better?

★ Will I ever find somebody who will love me?

★ Why does nobody like me?

★ Why do I get dissatisfied with everything I do?

★ Why can't I see things through?

★ What's for dinner?

★ Why am I here?

★ What is the point?

★ Why am I unhappy?

★ What's next?

Some of these questions are very empowering and others are disempowering. Even some of the ones that on the surface may seem to be empowering turn out not to be when you start to dig deeper. With any questions you come up with, ask yourself, 'What are the consequences of asking this question all the time?'

I used to have a question that I found myself asking again and again: 'How can I be part of this?' In other words, I was asking, 'What's happening and am I in on it?' At first that seemed like a great question because it opened up many opportunities. When something came along I would want to be part of it. I knew that I could find exciting new avenues and different ways to develop my life by being part of various different groups and by getting involved with countless different ideas and projects. However, I also realized that by doing this I wasn't able to stay focused on the most important things in my life. So rather than having a conversation with somebody and being totally focused on them, I was more interested in the conversation that was taking place behind them. I was wondering what was happening, and should I be involved with this conversation or that one? I also realized that 'How can I be part of this?' was actually disempowering. As soon as I understood this and how disempowering it could become, I changed my question.

To change my Life Question, I spent time thinking about what was important to me, the skills I had and the person I am. My new question became 'How can I use my unstoppable energy to stay focused on my life's mission?'

As soon as I got this new question into my mind I started to become more and more focused. Many opportunities would come along but, by continually asking that question, I realized that I could stay focused on the most important things. I made better choices, I wrote this book! I made better decisions and, most importantly, I didn't feel like I was missing out if I wasn't involved in everything.

So back to the question, 'What is your Life Question?' What's the question that you ask more than any other? A great way to look at this is to think, 'When I wake up each morning, what am I saying to myself? When I travel to go to work or go about those routine daily tasks, what am I asking myself?

At this point don't worry too much if something doesn't leap to mind. What I would like you to do is to become aware that there is a question. It may be that long after you've read this book the question will suddenly pop into your head.

When you discover your Life Question, ask yourself this: *Is this question an empowering question or a disempowering one?* If it's an empowering question, great. Keep asking it or even improve on it. Intensify it and ask that question more often. If it is a disempowering question, or it doesn't serve you, or doesn't take you to the place where you really want to get to, then change it to a new question. Then ask yourself that new question consciously throughout your day. Soon it will become part of your subconscious and that means it's a part of you.

If you're still not sure, here are some of the most common Life Questions I've heard over the years. Ask yourself if you think they are empowering or disempowering:

★ What's next?

★ What should I wear?

★ How did I end up doing this?

★ Is there more to life than this?

★ What's happening on Facebook?

★ How will X feel about this?

★ What's for tea?

★ Why does it always happen to me?

★ How can I fix this?

I would suggest that all of the above are disempowering at one level or another. So how about a list to spur you into writing a new, empowering, Life Question?

★ How can I use my talents for the greater good?

★ What can I do to make this moment even better?

★ Where can I find out more to motivate my mind and spur on my spirit?

- ★ What can I do today to grow?
- ★ What should I choose to feel?

Values

Now let's focus on your values. To start, you'll take a look at your values right now. Then you're going to look at whether they're the right values for you. Next you are going to explore whether you may want to change those values and how you can make them a key part of your life by creating new rules to support them.

Let's make it easy. First the guidelines. You must be totally honest as you go through this process because, if you don't, you will find that you are kidding yourself and shortly afterwards you will realize that the values you identified are not the most important ones to you. It's like going to a slimming club. You can tell yourself you are doing well, but the evidence will be seen at the weekly weigh-in. If you are doing this process with somebody else, it's likely that your values will be different from that person's. Remember, they are your values; there's no right or wrong answer. It's about what's important to you and about where you ultimately want to go in your life.

So let's start by asking the question: what are your current values? Not what you would *like* them to be, but what your current values are right now. How do you live your life? Let me give you some ideas of things you might consider to be values:

- ★ **Success.** Do you want to be successful? Do you want to lead the field? Do you want to be number one?
- ★ **Fun.** Do you have fun as one of your values? Do you want to laugh and enjoy life to the absolute full?
- ★ **Passion.** Is that something that you are excited about? Do you really want to experience huge passion in everything you do, so you'll go the extra mile and do whatever it takes?
- ★ **Greed.** Could you have greed as a value? Absolutely. If you think, 'Yes, I want more, more, more, more' then you can have greed as a value.
- ★ **Enthusiasm.** Do you leap out of bed, and run through your day with so much enthusiasm that you are going to knock the socks off people?
- ★ **Power.** Is power important to you? Do you want to lead in a way that people look at you and say, 'She is the most important person in this room.'
- ★ **Love.** Is love one of your values? To love other people and to be loved? Are loving relationships really important to you?

★ **Integrity/honesty.** Do you believe that truth is high on your list of values? Do you tell it how it is even if there are consequences? Do you feel mortally wounded when others betray this value?

★ **Recognition.** Do you want to be recognized for the work that you have done? Do you want people to acknowledge the contribution that you make? Do you want to be recognized for who, where and, most importantly, what you are doing?

★ **Rejection.** You may wonder how on earth you could have rejection as a value, but some people do, because that is an important part of their lives. They worry about it. The fear of rejection is right at the forefront. Something they would think about every single day. When it is that prevalent, then it is a value.

★ **Control.** Do you want to be in control? Do you know what you want and are you willing to do anything to ensure that's what happens? If you're a hands-on sort of a person and getting your way matters, then control could be a value.

★ **Blame.** Do you find yourself blaming others for situations that occur around you? Do you want to know who is causing the problem so you can 'get to the bottom of it'?

★ **Excitement.** Are you the type of person who jumps off cliffs with a hang-glider (or without one!)? Do you love to go on expeditions, or really want to take risks and go for it in an exciting way? Or do you look for excitement within the work that you do? Do you think that excitement is vital within relationships? Could it be one of your values?

★ **Security.** The antithesis of excitement. Do you want to be secure? Do you want to know exactly where everything is going to be on a regular basis? Do you want to come home and know what's what? Do you love that feeling of total security?

★ **Worry.** Do you find yourself worrying all the time? Do you have a habit of finding things to be concerned about? Then worry could be a value.

★ **Contribution.** Do you believe that contribution is critical? Do you want to give your time and resources to help others without any recognition? Are you the first to volunteer – even for the nasty jobs?

★ **Health.** Are you focused on your health? Do you watch carefully what you eat, focusing on really taking care of yourself, believing that nourishment and vitality are the key to the quality of life?

★ **Creativity.** Do you look to be creative in all that you do? Are you constantly thinking of new ways to do things? Do you believe it is important to think differently and move the boundaries? Do you love to see the results of your creative activities?

There are many different types of value. I would like you to stop reading for a moment and write down what you believe are your values. You can write down as many or as few as you like. Think carefully for a moment about what your current values are. Not what you would *like* them to be, but what your current values are right now.

Be totally **honest** and start **writing**

I hope you did write those values down, because this is one of the most important parts of this whole book and you are about to find out why.

To do this successfully you must follow the instructions carefully and really play full out with me. If you didn't write down your values then stop reading and do it now. Maybe you have started to think of other extra values that you can add to your list. That's fine – keep adding to it. You may or may not like the descriptions that I gave earlier for some of those other values. Remember, the values written earlier in the previous pages are not necessarily yours; they were just examples. So any word, any descriptions you use are entirely up to you.

The next thing I'd like you to do is to put the values in an order of impor-tance. Go through your list asking, 'Which is the most important value that I have on that list at this moment, *now*?' Not which one would you like it to be. When you have decided which one it's going to be, write the number 1 next to that value. Then identify the second most important. That doesn't mean that when you write number 2 that value isn't as important; it just means you are looking at things in detail to decide the order they should go in. This is your values list as it stands right now. Just rank them 1 through to 5 or 1 through to 10, however many values you might have. Do this now.

At this moment, you should have a list of values, and have them in an order starting with number 1 and going through to however many values you may have listed.

BRILL BIT

How many people do you know who have ever consciously thought about their values, bothered to write them down and put them in order? You have!

Here's another important question. What type of person do you ultimately want to become? Think carefully about this for a moment. It's not a question that we ask ourselves very often. Now – very specifically – write down a description (this can be pages if needs be, but it will be more than just a few words) of the type of person you would ultimately want to become. As before, stop reading and do it now.

Now that you've decided the type of person you ultimately want to become and written it down, I have one more question. Look at your list of current values and ask, 'Do these values, in this order, allow me to achieve my ultimate destiny?' Think very carefully about this for a moment. 'Do *these values*, in *this order* allow me to *achieve* my ultimate destiny?' You may be asking, 'Why is this so important?' It's simple. If your values are incongruent with the type of person you ultimately want to become, then it will be impossible for you to become that person.

I often work with people who say how much they would love to be known as a person who contributes massively to society, who gives their all to their family lives, who cares about the people around them. Then they look back at their list and see that values 1, 2 and 3 are power, recognition and risk. Do these values in this order allow them to achieve their ultimate destiny?

About 95 per cent of people who do this exercise properly realize that one of the reasons they are not achieving their ultimate destiny – why they are not truly satisfied with their lives – is because their value system is either completely wrong, some part of the list is wrong, or the values are in the wrong order. When they look at their value system they understand for the first time that their values in their current order will not allow them to become all they want to become.

Creating your new values

This is an exciting time in your journey to being brilliant. Yes, you may have found something that is wrong, but now you know exactly where you are in your life and you can replace, change and tweak. You can also add new rules, rules which are going to help you to achieve your ultimate destiny fast!

Just think about this for a moment. Right now you're at an exact moment when your life will never be the same again. I don't know about you, but I'm excited as I write this; I hope you share that excitement as you read it! You may be thinking 'OK, I'll redo my values later.' If that's you, please don't do it later; do it right now! Your life will change in positive ways for you right now by taking the correct actions in the next few moments.

Whether you need to change, replace or just tweak your values, here's what you need to do to create a new value system for yourself.

Ask yourself this: *'In order to become the type of person that I ultimately want to become, what type of values would a person like that have?'* Just focus now on that person and ask what values they would have. Now I'm going to ask you to write these values down – really explore this, almost like a brainstorm.

Once you've done this, choose your words very carefully, because these words are going to be very empowering to you. These words are going to be ones that you will use to shape your destiny. These words are going to be the ones that will get you up in the morning and will help you to make decisions throughout your life. Every single day these words will come into your mind. Take time now to imagine the type of person you ultimately want to become and what that person's values would be.

The next stage is exactly as you did before. Go through your list, decide if they are truly the values that you really want to have in order to become that person who you ultimately want to become. Once you have chosen the ones that are most important, put them in order. Then ask yourself the question: 'Do these values, in this order, allow me to achieve my ultimate destiny?' When you look at your new list and think about the question, can you say 'Yes' from your heart? If you can answer 'Yes' with a passion and a total certainty, then you know that this new values list is going to be your guiding compass that will lead you to your ultimate destiny.

Now what if you look at your new list and you say, 'Yeah, they're OK'? If this is the case then your values are not coming from a place of passion and certainty and from your heart. Dig deep down, dig really deep and ask yourself, truly now, truly, 'Do those values, in this order, allow me to achieve my ultimate destiny?' If the answer is 'No', then get back to work and do them again.

Right, now you should have a new values list. Do you think living those values should be difficult or easy? I think you'll want to make living and feeling those values as easy as possible.

Take a step back for a moment and think about how you created your original value system. Before you wrote down your values, how did they become values to you? They only become values, true values, when you lived them. When you lived them every single day. Think about how you create a value in the first place – you're not born with them. Whether you are conscious of the process or not, you decide what is important to you, then you create a belief system to support that, then you find the evidence to support that belief system. They are the rules to support your value. Who made the rules? Who made the rules that gave you the values that you *used* to have?

You did!

If one of your values was recognition, there's probably a time you could go back to in your life when recognition was not there. A time came along when recognition was important and you thought, 'Yeah, I feel good about this. I want to be recognized for what I do.' You made it important. You also decided what the rules were going to be. Your rules for recognition may be that you want to have something written down in a letter from somebody, or in a card saying what a great job you've done. Somebody else might have recognition as one of their values and all they need is a kind word from somebody. Somebody else may have recognition and all it needs is an appreciative look. You create the rules. You create the rules that fit the belief system. The belief system forms the value.

Take a look at the new values list you have. Now think about the *new rules* that you can create to help you to live those new values every single day. Here's a tip: make it easy for yourself!

Let's take the value of 'fun'. Your first rule could be, 'I have fun every time I hear laughter'. Notice it's not 'every time I laugh'. 'Every time I hear laughter' will allow you to experience the value of fun more often. What if you decided to feel the value of fun every time you see a bright colour? Could you do that?

Remember, you made the rules so you can change them and make new rules. If you should decide, 'I'm going to enjoy life a little more every time it starts to rain', you can!

Perhaps a final example here could be the value of success. How do you measure success? For some people the rules are simple. 'When I'm number one, when I'm absolutely certain that I've done every single thing that I could ever do to achieve every bit of success in my life, that's when I'm going to feel the success value. When my salary hits a certain point, that's when I'll know I've been successful. When I'm driving a certain car, that's how I'll know I've been successful. I'm successful when I'm hitting £x in sales. When my kids tell me I've done this, when my friends recognize me for doing that, that's when I'll feel successful.'

That's all well and good but when will they ever truly feel success? They probably never will feel true success because they are always pushing themselves to the next level. This is great in terms of goals, but remember, I want you to live these values, I want you to *feel* these values, every day. So if you have a value of success, how about saying instead:

★ I feel success every time I turn up somewhere on time.

★ I feel success every time I get to the end of the day and I have connected with other people and made them happy.

★ I feel success every time that I feel certain about any project I am working on in my life.

★ I feel success every time I see my kids smile because I created them.

★ I feel success every time I look out in the world and see other people being successful.

Create those as your success rules and you will feel success every day! Here's the best bit, you become more successful day by day because you changed the value system and you changed the rules.

This exercise is one that could be easier for some people. What I would like you to do is stop reading for a moment and really concentrate on the rules that you're going to create to go with each value. These are the rules that you will create to support your new value system. They will allow you to become the type of person you would ultimately want to become. So stop reading and do it now.

Congratulations! You have done something that very few people ever take an opportunity to do with their lives. You have created a new values system. You have shaped the rules to fit with that values system. The next stage is to live that values system. Writing it down is an exciting process. Living it is the most exciting thing you could ever choose to do.

BRILL BIT

Create a visual image of your new value system and the new rules. Make sure you look at it every single day. Fill your mind with these values. Work on them. Adjust them. Change them if you need to, and ask yourself questions about the type of person that you would ultimately want to become.

I know for many people this is the most exciting part of this book. It can be challenging to understand. You may need to read this chapter several times to get a deep understanding. Please work hard and endeavour to create a value system that will empower you. If you do, your life will never ever be the same again.

So far we have focused the brilliance message on you. But let me ask you a question. Do you at any point in your life have to work with or spend time with other human beings? Thought so. Well, in order for you to be the very best in these situations, you have to know how to create …

TEN YEARS ON

I was coaching a very kind and big-hearted person recently. One of his values is to be 'generous', which sounds, and is, wonderful (particularly when you're on the receiving end). In fact, he's the type of person everyone wants to be around because of his generous and caring nature.

You can tell I'm about to say 'but'. And it's a BIG but.

His rules for being generous weren't clear. He felt the best way to embody his generous nature was to spend money or give things away (even when he couldn't afford to).

He'd read *How to Be Brilliant* a couple of years before we first met and he showed me his values list. We reviewed his Life Question, values and rules. Here's where we were both surprised: in just two years his values had changed slightly and his Life Question had changed totally. It became: 'How can I make this person/moment/event feel better and be better for me?'

The big change was his rules for the value of generosity. Rather than only feeling the value of being generous when he spent money on people, he changed it to: 'I feel generous every time someone says thank you, I'm kind, polite or caring'.

I remember travelling home that day thinking about my values and realizing mine had changed too.

The lesson here is simple, and read this twice:

Values can change you, just as you can change your values.

BRILLIANT TEAMS

You must have heard it a million times: TEAM – **T**ogether **E**veryone **A**chieves **M**ore. I'm sure they do but let's get a little self-centred for a moment and think how brilliant teams may benefit you. Much of this chapter is work focused but all the ideas are transferable into other areas of life where you'll find yourself among a group of people.

Can you remember a time when you have been part of a brilliant team? Was it during school or in your first job? Was it a community project or a drama production? Perhaps it was a sports team or a special workforce. Have you ever felt lucky to have been part of a team where the whole was so much greater than the sum of the parts? Then good news, this chapter will help you remove the luck and create brilliant teams whenever you need them.

And guess what? In just 90 days it's possible to build a team (if you don't have one already), improve your teamwork, complete a project, learn from the project, dismantle the team – and have a whole lot of fun along the way.

What makes the perfect team?

'Choose people in a team who don't really get on, they will stretch each other.' Ever heard that one? Who comes up with this stuff? Choose people who may give different opinions, but if you are building the team from scratch yourself, then don't choose people you don't like! Think about a time when a person who you really admired, who you rated as good or better than yourself and who you respected or loved, has given a different opinion. Now think about a person who you don't really like, who rubs you up the wrong way, who has different values from your own and imagine them giving you a different opinion. Now choose who you want on your team. Incidentally, you'd still feel the same way about them even if they agreed with you!

The trick is to find people **who complement each other** rather than putting up with those who detract

Think of a football (that's soccer to some) team; 11 goal keepers might share skill sets but it would be a terrible team. What about an amazingly skilful goalkeeper who has had a personal challenge with the equally talented defenders? They don't communicate and what happens? They lose!

So here's a thought. Write down the characteristics you'd like to see in a perfect team. If you are putting together a new team for yourself, this will be an exciting challenge because you'll also be able to develop your team along these criteria. If you are a member of a team, or going to be a member of a team, still do it!

BRILL BIT

If you are putting together a team at work, write 'ads' for the type of people you are looking for in the same style you would see in the newspaper recruitment pages. Leave the ads on people's desks. One may look a little like this:

CLASSIFIEDS

Lorem ipsum dolor sit amet, consectetuer adipiscing elit, sed diam nonummy nibh

Completer Finisher Required

Internal auditing require a talented person to join a new team with the task of reducing errors on internal transactions.The successful applicant will love pulling ideas together and implementing them rapidly.

Hours : 3 per week
Pay : normal salary plus
unlimited tea and biscuits at meetings!

FOR MORE INFORMATION TALK TO:
SUE SMITH EXTENSION 434.

Lorem ipsum dolor sit amet, consectetuer

So now let's assume you have recruited your brilliant team. Give them some oomph! I'm going to focus on the workplace for this section, but remember these rules are transferable.

How many times have you sat down in a meeting with a new team and the leader has started with a dull, dull, dull ramble about what you are going to do? Test this out instead. Make a bold statement about this new team using key words to describe how you want it to be: outstanding, best, imaginative, funky, fun, rapid etc. Then ask who would like to be part of a team like this. If anyone says 'No', ask them for an alternative or suggest they move to a different team! Your leadership will be measured as much by your inability to get rid of poor performers as it will be for recruiting good ones!

Spend a few minutes developing a set of rules and make sure they are neatly typed up. One set is printed on *dayglo* paper signed by everyone on the team and laminated (to take to every meeting) and the others are passed out. It all sounds very practical so far and, with these little tips, you should start to create a good team, but remember, good can create poor results. So what needs to happen to make a team brilliant?

Here are the five steps to making any team brilliant. And just in case you were thinking, 'I'm not a team leader, I can't do that', change your language, become a leader, and step up to brilliance – the rest will soon follow!

1 Total immersion and mastery

Total immersion is the very best way to learn anything. I had a friend who went to driving lessons for an hour every week for three years but didn't pass her test until she'd been on a one-week intensive driving course. After three years of dabbling, at the end of the intensive week she passed her test. Look at the stats: even with cancellations, bad weather and holidays she had 40 lessons per year = 120 hours over 3 years – and failed to even take a test. On her intensive course she drove for a maximum of 25 hours but passed first time.

Mastery comes when you truly understand your subject. Imagine a team of five people who are all committed to mastering their project or task. How would it feel to be held to a higher level by those around you? Mastery sets that standard.

2 Know your outcome

How will you know when you've been successful? More teams start on projects without clear outcomes than ever before. Meetings take hours, reporting is slow, and worst of all you don't know if you've been successful.

By defining clear outcomes early on, you know your target. Actually that's what fantastic teams do. Brilliant teams create great language around those outcomes. They tell others their plans to be accountable, and write them down as goals using the three Ps (**P**ersonal, **P**ositive and **P**resent tense) to ensure they are driven towards achieving their goal.

3 Focus

Where your focus goes, energy flows. Steve Walker was the Chief Executive Officer of AmicusHorizon – a (now) highly successful social housing provider. When Steve took the reins the organization was in supervision (the last step before they would be closed). He created a clear vision for the whole organization and communicated it to every member of staff: achieve three stars in three years (the highest achievement for their sector) and become a *Sunday Times* top 100 company to work for. Ask any member of the almost 1,000 strong staff about the goals of the organization and they will tell you. They know exactly what they are there to do. Everything else leads from these key goals. At every meeting the question is asked, 'Will this action take us closer to our goals or move us further away?'

4 Pace – West Wing teams!

I loved the American drama series *The West Wing*; it gave a glimpse of what it's like to run the USA from the famous West Wing of the White House. In each episode President Bartlett, brilliantly played by Martin Sheen, runs an amazing team of advisors, experts, directors and assistants who make rapid decisions and carry out plans with brutal speed. Even though it's 'just TV', I brought the same ideas into my organization with amazing results. I've been raving about West Wing speed, West Wing teams and West Wing meetings ever since!

West Wing speed means you accelerate everything you do by 50 per cent. Yes 50 per cent! But you must do it in the context of the team. The key is to get everyone moving at the same speed from the moment they come into the workplace until they go home. You don't have to be the manager to do this (in many ways it's better if you aren't), but you must keep up the momentum.

West Wing teams rely on the fact that the team is always right, even when you're wrong! Let me explain. The team can dissect, criticize, admit defeat, moan and groan all they like but to the outside world you are always one unit, defending every action and making the most out of every situation. Politics at the highest level can be tumbled by the smallest crack. So can your team!

West Wing meetings are my favourite. Let me begin by telling you what they *don't* do when having a team meeting in *The West Wing.* They don't:

★ Arrive 10 minutes late.

★ Dawdle into the room.

★ Start the meeting by finding out 'who wants tea and who wants coffee'.

★ Chat about what they did at the weekend.

★ Set up a PowerPoint presentation.

★ Apologize for not having enough copies of the 28-page report.

★ Tap a teacup to get attention.

★ Spend the first five minutes deciding who will take notes.

★ Ever say 'We'll park it till next week'.

★ Say 'Look at the time – we've been in here for hours. Should we send out for sandwiches because Terry hasn't started his presentation yet and Sue still needs to bottom-out our policy on the new strategy for Q3? But we'll have to move rooms because Gavin and his team of 30 need this room at 12 to do an analysis on VAT implications on expenses during the Q2. So let's take a vote on who wants to move rooms or who wants to put off the presentation from Terry and Sue's agenda item until next week. But before we do that, can I just have a quick indication again, who wants tea and who wants coffee …?'

In West Wing team meetings the team members are like this:

★ They all stand. Yes STAND – I love this!

★ They give a brief (less than 15 seconds) résumé of their opinion.

★ They have 30 seconds to debate a decision.

★ They make a decision (or the President does!).

★ They take immediate action on the decision whilst walking back to their desks.

The whole thing is done in five minutes. Brilliant!

5 Take massive immediate action on every decision

Brilliant teams get things done. It's that simple. Teams break down, become ineffective, and ultimately fail because of many factors, all of which can be overcome by taking massive immediate action. When you're busy taking the correct actions, you can achieve masses. The key is *immediate*. Procrastination is the thin end of the wedge that removes the momentum.

There are some great books on procrastination, but as I'm worried that you'll never get round to reading them, here are seven quickies to overcome team procrastination:

★ **Set worthwhile goals that intensely motivate.** It's a given that if the goals motivate the team then the team is more likely to take action. See Chapter 3 for more details.

★ **Visualize the task as completed.** Imagine starting a team project by asking everyone to close their eyes and visualize the project completed. Seeing the outcomes exactly as they want. Then get them to link this emotionally and anchor the feeling by using the image.

★ **Affirmations – do it now!** This one needs some guts but if you can get your team mates to use this simple powerful affirmation, 'Do it now', it really does get teams to take action. At the end of a brief West Wing meeting cry out, 'When are we going to do it?' 'DO IT NOW!' should be the instant response.

★ **Put your team on record**. It's amazing what a little bit of visibility will do to encourage people to take action. Our project *will* be completed by the end of the month. Tell everyone – then it's a must.

★ **Refuse to make excuses/rationalize.** 'Well we would have got started sooner but we had too many other things to do.' I bet you wish you had a cash bonus every time you heard those words! By refusing to make excuses, you will make your and your team's actions immediate.

★ **Create a reward system for yourselves.** Will everyone get a bar of chocolate for completing phase 1 or will it be a night out on completion? Why not set up a reward fund (don't spend hours discussing it – do it or don't).

★ **Overpower the biggest task first.** It feels great when you conquer a big Rock and as a team you feel unstoppable. Use the techniques in 'Brilliant rock-busting' (Chapter 6) to get this done.

Massive immediate action can be increased using lots of methods, but the best I have found come from creative use of music. Music gives immediate anchors to moments from our past (mostly positive) that help us to move into an emotional state very quickly. Take time to find some motivating music to inspire you and your team, and it doesn't have to be the over-used 'Simply the Best'!

Ending teams

The final part of brilliant teams is knowing when and how to dismantle the team. So often teams are left to simply fall apart. Great movies have a start, middle and an end. Often the movie ending is the best part. Teams on the other hand have great starts, get weak in the middle and drift off in the end.

So it's worth taking a look at what you can do to end teams in a classy way. If you're working on a 90-day massive action plan I would suggest you keep the last few days for tidying. If you have recruited a 'completer finisher' (or if you are that person), get everyone to feed back to them what they have done and actions completed. Then document it. You don't need huge reports, just get it all brought together with a few notes about what happened, when and by whom. Pull together the data and ask at the final meeting the three critical questions:

1 What did we set out to achieve?

2 Did we achieve it?

3 If so, how? If not, why not?

That's it. Make the final report easy for someone in the future to pick up, use and learn from. Then you're on to a winner.

Each part of the 'Brilliant teams' chapter can be accelerated to the power of 10 or more by adding one more ingredient. It is ...

TEN YEARS ON

The original manuscript for *How to Be Brilliant* didn't have this chapter. I was asked to write it as my Editor thought the book needed a chapter on teams. How right she was.

West Wing team meetings have become commonplace in many organizations, and meetings that used to last an age are thankfully a thing of the past.

In fact, it's more important than ever to build effective teams that can get tasks done quickly. The days of an eight-hour meeting are over (or should be); I bet you could get exactly the same amount done in 75 per cent of the time.

BRILL BIT

Meetings normally last for an hour because that's what people schedule for them. I challenge you to make your next (normally one-hour) meeting just 45 minutes, and I bet you get the same amount done.

There's nothing else I need to say on brilliant teams, so in the spirit of West Wing meetings – next!

10

BRILLIANT VISION

How would it feel if you knew 100 per cent, in your heart, that you could achieve anything you put your mind to? In order to create that level of certainty, your vision for brilliance must become part of your life every moment of every day. It's time to learn how to do this and to do it in several ways.

The first stage is very simple and lots of fun. Spend some time putting together a visual representation of how life will look when you have *achieved* your goal. In the most basic form you can draw a picture (a stick man picture would do) of you achieving brilliance in the area you want. However, with a little time and effort, you can find and cut pieces out of magazines, take photographs and or get images from the internet.

Say you have a goal that you want to visit Florida. And why not? Spend some time finding a really strong visual representation of how it would look when you have achieved the goal. You've got to get creative here. If you think, 'Wait a minute, how can I have a picture of me in Florida when I've never been outside Newcastle?', you will quickly limit your options. This is about using your imagination and being creative. Go to a travel agent, get a brochure, find a great picture, take a photo of yourself (with the people who you want to be there with) and stick it in the picture – you with Mickey Mouse would be great! If it isn't Mickey Mouse that floats your boat then get something that represents Florida. Whether it's the coastline, the Kennedy Space Center or Disneyland, find something that would represent Florida for you.

If you have a brilliance goal – for example, being brilliant at managing a team – then create an image that sums this up for you. Would you be receiving an award? Could you get pictures of your team and have them with speech bubbles saying what a brilliant team leader you are? Don't worry, you won't be pinning it to the notice board or leaving it on your desk.

What if you have a goal to be in peak physical fitness? Put your head on somebody else's body if you need to. Whatever it takes – just get a great visual representation. Creating images like this could take you five minutes, it may take an hour or even a half day, but it's a great experience and it starts the visioning process. Then put them into a nice book – the type you would like to carry around. This means it's easy to have the image with you at all times.

You can do this in many creative ways. The actor Jim Carrey wrote himself a cheque for $10 million in 1990 when he was broke. He post-dated it for

Thanksgiving 1995 – just five years in the future, and carried it with him at all times. Just a few weeks before the target date he signed a deal to star in *Dumb and Dumber*. His fee? $10 million!

The **image** is powerful but so are the **words** that go with it

The next stage is to write the affirmation that goes with each picture. Remember to make it personal, make it positive and put it into the present tense: the three Ps. You can start by writing: I am, I have, I own or whatever it is. To go back to that holiday in Florida, you could write down, 'I am having the most amazing holiday of my lifetime in Florida now'. Not, 'One day in the future I'd like to go to Florida.' How woolly is that? How vague is that? Would Muhammad Ali have said that? No! If you want to go to Florida, then the way you're going to get there is through massive action and programming your brain to believe you are achieving it now, creating Gestalt. See a picture of you and your family and visualize them in the exact situation you want to be, then write down your affirmation with passion. If you need some inspiration, go back to Chapter 3.

If you want to be a brilliant team leader then clearly write the words: 'I am a brilliant team leader now.' If you want to be financially free, then create an image of yourself being financially free. That may mean a zero balance on a credit card bill or a healthy bank account. Create the image that works, then write down: 'I am financially free now.' If you want to have incredible health, create the image and write down, 'I am in peak physical health now.' Do this with each of your goals.

The third step is to state by when you will achieve this goal. Decide on the date. Then write this date next to the goal that is to be achieved. Go through each of them and, just as Jim Carrey did, write down the date.

BRILL BIT

Don't be tempted to write, 'in one week', 'in two months' or 'in a year's time' etc. because every time you look at that goal and read that timescale it will still be a week, two months or a year away. You need an actual real date, such as 'by 1st June'.

A goal is just a dream without a date on it.

Here's a note of caution. One of the things people tend to do is over-estimate how much they can achieve in the short term and under-estimate how much they can achieve in the long term. Be careful to get the balance right.

If you set a goal and it doesn't work out exactly how you intended it to, or if it takes a little bit longer to achieve, don't worry – it doesn't matter. The fact that you are now on the journey, the fact that you have now stepped up, that you have made a commitment towards achieving the goal is something 99 per cent of people never do. You are on the way – that's the important thing. Enjoy the journey, go for it and make a commitment.

The next stage of the process is to build on the visual image you have created and use it to completely replace any negativity or self-doubt that these things couldn't happen. To do this you will create an image in your mind and do so with such a passion and enthusiasm that it becomes real.

The best way to do this is, every morning, when you first wake up, sit up and read your goals. Every night when you go to bed read your goals. Make smaller visual versions of goals and put a copy into your wallet or purse. Stick them on to your mirror so you see them several times a day. Really believe that you have achieved those goals, visualize yourself completing them, and you are then more likely to achieve them.

BRILL BIT

Here's a cracker from Jeffrey Gitomer. He calls it 'Achieve your goals with Post-it® Notes'. Write down your big goals in three to five words. Put them on the bathroom mirror where you will see them at least twice a day. Keep looking at and reading them and you will begin to take action. Just seeing the note there every day makes you act on it. When a goal has been completed, add new ones. You may want to transfer your achieved goals to the inside door of your wardrobe – that way you can revisit your success every day while dressing!

But what if I don't achieve all my goals? 'I'm frightened I'll fail.' Have you ever heard yourself saying that? Have you ever just not attempted something in case you fail? If you don't give at least one major goal a go I can guarantee you something – you won't achieve any. However, what if you go for five and only achieve four? You're already four times more successful than the someone who didn't take the first step.

Sometimes people say, 'I've set 10 great goals and I achieved 8. They then beat themselves up because they didn't achieve the other two. I have a belief system which is, 'The best for all concerned will occur'. Sometimes people aren't ready to achieve a certain goal. People aren't ready to be at a certain place. Sometimes it might affect somebody else in an adverse way. So remember this when you set your goals: the best for all concerned *will* occur. If you have the passion, the enthusiasm, the excitement for your goals, then many more are going to be achieved than fall by the wayside.

I know you will achieve your goals as long as you have lashings of the final ingredient – MASSIVE ACTION!

This all sounds very exciting but what about the practical actions that are needed day by day? You know, just getting up and looking at the goals and reading them is a bit like, 'No weeds, no weeds'. It's action that makes the difference.

A powerful and simple action you can take to help with your vision is to mentally run through the actions you need to take towards achieving your goals. This is called mental rehearsal. Mental rehearsal is used by all top performers in a variety of ways. You can often see athletes mentally rehearsing on the track before they run a race, or you can see golfers mentally rehearsing before they take their swing.

By mentally rehearsing something, you are preparing your whole physiology from your brain to the tips of your toes for the activity that you're about to embark on. So, when it comes to achieving your vision, what could you mentally rehearse?

Here's a list of some of the popular activities people mentally rehearse:

Communication	Other areas
Interviews	Finding a parking space
Presentations	A night out
Meetings	Golf swing
Reviews	Sporting event
A telephone conversation	Writing a letter or report
Handling a complaint	A journey
Asking for help	

I want to give you an example of how mental rehearsal works and the power of your brain. This works brilliantly with your eyes closed, so if you can, get someone to read this to you. If not, use your imagination as you read, taking breaks if you want to feel each part.

Imagine that it is the hottest day of the year. It's sweltering. The temperature has been building up throughout the day and around about midday you decide to go out for a long walk. It's a really great experience as you pace along enjoying your walk. After a few hours, you realize that your mouth is very dry, so dry that you feel you have a tongue like an old sock. The most important thing you want right now is a drink but there's nowhere you can get one. The only option is to walk home. As you are walking home your mouth gets drier and drier – you're desperate to get a drink.

Eventually you reach your front door. You walk into the house and no one else is home. You walk into the kitchen and think 'I must get a drink now.' You open the fridge, look inside and you see a wonderful cold bottle of mineral water, still or sparkling, your choice. Imagine now that you take out the bottle and open it. You find a nice clean glass and start to pour the water.

Just before you pick up the glass you think, 'I'm going to be tidy,' so you put the bottle back into the fridge, and as you are doing so, you notice there's a lemon on the shelf. That lemon is perfect, with a wonderful bright yellow skin. Imagine now picking up the lemon; feel the waxiness of the skin. Wouldn't it be nice to have a little bit of lemon in that mineral water? You take a knife and slice the lemon in half. Then you take the knife and slice a half in half again. You take the quarter of lemon and you're just about to drop it in the glass. But, rather than putting it into the water, you bring it to your mouth and bite into it. Imagine now biting into that lemon. How does it taste? How does it smell?

Let's have a look at what happened there. It isn't the hottest day of the year. Well it might be, but the chances are it's not right now, as you're reading this book. However, the more that I talked about it getting hotter and hotter and the more that I described your mouth getting drier and drier, I'm sure your mouth did become drier. You probably began to move your tongue around and started to move your jaw trying to get some saliva into your mouth. Then when I talked about the lemon and biting into it saliva was released into your mouth.

Is it the hottest day? No! Was there a lemon? No! It was just in your imagination but you managed to get a physiological response. Your body has responded to something that you only imagined. So by imagining something first, could you get a better physical response when you go into the true situation? Absolutely!

I heard a great story about testing mental rehearsal with a basketball team, at UCLA in California. Researchers split the team into three groups. Then for phase one they got each player to throw 100 shots and measured how many baskets each team scored. For phase two they took the three groups and gave them different types of practice. The first group was a control group; they didn't do anything different at all. The second group completed an extra hour's practice every day just throwing at the basket. That is all they would do, shoot at the basket for that extra hour every single day. The third group just mentally rehearsed for an extra hour each day, all they did was practise in their mind's eye.

They brought the three teams back together one month later. As you would expect, the control group hadn't improved but the group that had practised for one hour every single day throwing the ball had improved, in fact they showed a good improvement. The most staggering outcome of all was the group who just mentally rehearsed. All they did was one extra hour of mental rehearsal each day but their scores were greater than any of the others!

This is because when they practised in their heads they never missed, so the pathways of brain cells formed into an 'accurate shooting' neurological pathway.

A further month later, the researchers brought the teams back together again. This time the group who had done an extra hour of physical practice every day had dropped their scores. However, the group who had just done mental rehearsal maintained higher scores.

BRILL BIT

The reason the team who had been mentally rehearsing maintained high scores for longer was they had practised hitting the basket *every single time*. Every shot was successful. So when it came to doing the exercise, they were 100 per cent sure in their minds that they could hit. Of course, not every single ball went in but over a month they had created a pathway of brain cells that was permanent.

Start to think about the things that you could mentally rehearse and how you could get the perfect outcomes you want.

Have you ever had to go to an important meeting where you needed to be prepared? You prepare your papers, you prepare where you're going to, you prepare transport, you get your directions, you set off in good time, but do you actually mentally prepare the meeting? With mental rehearsal you would see yourself in the meeting. You would hear the things that people were going to say. You would experience the whole feeling, the whole sensation of the meeting, before you even go through the door. Most importantly, you would see yourself being successful.

If you spent five minutes mentally rehearsing a meeting, would that meeting be more successful, less successful or exactly the same? My guess is it would be more successful. What if you were going to have a night out? Could you mentally rehearse having a great night out with friends? Of course you could. You could see yourself having a great time, meeting the right people, going to the right places, everybody getting along, having an amazing experience together.

Again ask the same question. If you spent five minutes mentally rehearsing having a great night out, would you have a better night out, a worse night out or would that night out be exactly the same? My guess is that you would have a better night out because of the experience that you have mentally rehearsed in your mind.

What about a presentation? What if you had to stand up and do a presentation in front of 500 people? I bet you're thinking, 'Oh no, I would never want to do a presentation in front of 5 people never mind 500!' But if you did, one of the great ways to prepare for a presentation is to mentally rehearse the process first. See yourself presenting brilliantly, receiving praise (a standing ovation even), see everybody nodding and cheerfully agreeing with what you are presenting. By doing that, do you think that you will have a better chance of making a great presentation?

What about in sport? If you play tennis or any other sport that requires hand-to-eye co-ordination, could you mentally practise making shots before you actually took them? Imagine how much better you would become!

Research carried out at Edinburgh University discovered that the brain processes information in much the same way in mental rehearsal as it does during actual physical activity. So, mental rehearsal can work in many different areas of your life. Use this tool. Test it out. It's a key part of creating a vision. Mental rehearsal is a very simple yet very powerful technique. A few minutes invested mentally rehearsing each important area of your life will pay back many times.

Now it's time to take massive actions, practical actions that are going to make a difference. Sorry folks, brilliance as a standard always equals some real hard work.

The first thing you are going to do is to break your vision into the 90-day blocks you discovered in Chapter 3. Take the very first goal on your list and say, 'OK, when do I intend to achieve this goal by?' It could be a 90-day goal or 6 months, 1 year, 5 years, 10 years. Whatever it's going to be, you to create momentum you need to take some action right here right now.

Have a look at your list and ask:

★ What do I need to achieve in the next 90 days to take me closer towards reaching that goal?

★ What do I need to have in place?

★ What must I have done for myself?

★ What resources do I need to have around me?'

Start asking these questions now as these are the key demands that make your plan.

Consider what resources you have right now and what resources you need to bring into your life towards achieving that goal. That resource could also be, 'Who do I know now who can help me?' One of the best ways to get help is by building rapport with people who you know can help you towards achieving the goals. Remember your Farm List?

The resources could be people or books, places or information, or it might be stuff you are going to do for yourself. Consider the different resources that need to be in place and write them down. And it's really important that you do write them down. I believe when you have written something you've made a commitment. You've made a commitment on paper but, more importantly, you have made a commitment to yourself . . .

This is what I'm going to do

Then the key is to schedule it. By making time, writing down the commitment and clearly defining when it becomes part of your 90-day massive action programme, it really has become a 90-day plan.

Now let's get this really started. What do you need to achieve in the next 30 days? Take a look at your list and identify either the things that will be completed or the actions that will have happened in the next 30 days.

Actually, if you are going to plan the next 30 days, why not plan the next 7? Commit to 7 days of massive action to really get the momentum started. By taking massive action for 7 days, the next 30 days are going to be easy. Take massive action for 30 days and the next 90 days are going to be even easier. Do this for 90 days and you're on a roll.

Now take out your diary and schedule with as much accuracy as possible when you will take the necessary actions. Do this and you are going to achieve your goals much faster than you ever thought possible. You will be brilliant!

Most people use their diaries or calendars only to schedule meetings or events not activities. You are not most people.

BRILL BIT

Five frogs were sitting on a log. One decides to jump off; how many are left?

The answer is five. Why? Because the frog only decided to jump off. It didn't actually schedule the jump time and stick to it!

Continue to follow this format: what will happen after the next 7 days? Or how about the next 24 hours? Think about this, whatever you do in the next 24 hours is going to springboard you towards the next 7 days, 30 days, 90 days, 1 year, 5 years, 10 years. Yes, the next 24 hours! You cannot put things off any longer. You have made a commitment so it's time to start it ... NOW. Take any actions. Just choose one or two things that you are actually going to do. Make that call. Go and see that person. Buy and read that book. Get whatever you need together. Talk to people. Make a commitment. Get out and take some exercise. Do something that will move you closer towards achieving your goal. Do it right now or at the latest in the next 24 hours. Schedule! Schedule! Schedule!

Finally, what are you going to do in the next 15 minutes? In the next 15 minutes you may have put down this book. That is the most critical time, because if you say, 'I enjoyed that; there were some great ideas in there and now I know them,' but you are not doing them, then you have wasted your precious time. Because, as I said right at the start of *How to Be Brilliant*, knowing something at an intellectual level is not enough. This is about the doing. This is about taking the actions. This is about making a difference now.

In the next few pages I'm going to ask you to make a decision. Whatever decision you make, I want you to promise yourself you are going to stick with it and move forwards with that decision. Tell yourself it's going to make a difference and it's going to last, not just for 5, 10 or 15 minutes, not just for a week, a month or a year. Commit to taking the actions that will change your life forever – starting right here right now.

In the future, if you look back at this time and you haven't taken the actions, think about what you could have missed out on. Think about what you could miss out on now by not following through. Now tell yourself, 'This is not a should or a could, it's a must. I'm going to take the actions and I'm going to start right now.' Are you ready to live your life like that?

If you are ready, you can make a commitment to yourself and you can test that level of commitment by putting ...

TEN YEARS ON

I've talked a lot about scheduling in this chapter, and I firmly believe that the No.1 reason behind the success or failure to achieve your goals is action.

In the past 10 years, the mechanism that could have assisted your 'brilliant vision' might have been the very thing that crippled it. I'm talking about technology.

Now it's commonplace to schedule a task on your desktop and have it prompt you via your mobile device. We live in a world of emails, texts and instant messaging. We can even make video calls from a small device that fits in our pocket. Do you remember watching old sci-fi films where a robot would bring the owner the phone? Now the robot IS the phone!

The challenge is, that same device is full of procrastination-powered distractions. Social media was designed to 'connect' people yet it saps hours from their lives. Millions of people now watch TV, 'attend' meetings and eat with family and friends with their 'second screen' in hand and in sight.

I'm not writing this to tell you what you should or shouldn't be doing with your technology or time. But I am asking you to think very carefully about what you spend your time focusing on and to answer this question: 'Will the activity I am participating in right now take me closer to or move me further away from my ultimate vision?'

Written goals

My biggest change of heart/mind comes in the form of written goals. I've read hundreds of personal development books and it has always been a constant message: write your goals – if you don't, you'll never achieve your vision.

I really believed that was the best way to set goals. Then, a few years ago, we started a major research project that involved interviewing highly successful achievers from all walks of life. One of the questions we asked them was, 'Do you set goals?'.

You won't be surprised to learn that almost every one said they did. We then asked, 'Are your goals written?'. And this was where we got the shock. Of those we interviewed, 90 per cent DIDN'T have written goals.

It didn't mean they weren't as committed, couldn't see the outcome or didn't visualize their completed goals (using present tense), it's just they didn't feel the need to write them down.

So, make up your own mind when it comes to your vision. If you want to write it down, go for it. If you just want to visualize it and create powerful imagery, that's great too.

The only option that is not an option is not creating a vision and just hoping for a brilliant future.

When it comes to creating a vision, hope is not a strategy.

11

BRILLIANCE INTO ACTION

Time for a review

can't say it often enough: massive action = massive results. Now it's time to put everything you have learned into action.

> *'Vision without action is a daydream. Action without vision is a nightmare.'* (JAPANESE PROVERB)

Let's take all the ideas you've absorbed so far and see how you can apply them now to create your amazing, incredible future.

A quick recap

First of all your Wheel of Life is designed to point out the areas where you must take massive action. Use the Wheel of Life on a regular basis, at least once a month. You can also use it to plot your progress and make sure your life is balanced and that you're thinking about everything – it's a simple yet effective tool.

★ **Use the characteristics of brilliant people.** Practise positive language, positive belief and positive action, in a way that engages you.

★ **Break out of your comfort zone.** The things that hold other people back will never hold you back again. Use pace, team and fun.

★ **Think differently.** Now that you understand more about how your brain works, apply those ideas, reprogramme your brain and consciously send your thoughts in the right direction.

★ **Learn how to manage stress.** Use relaxation on a regular basis to get to that alpha–theta level.

★ **Take massive action.** Remember, massive action = massive results. Do it now!

Follow those principles and you will see a rapid difference in the quality of your life. Remember, by making a decision and stepping up in the areas that you think are the most important in your life, you are being brilliant. You can focus on many areas for goals but go for a maximum of three for brilliance.

Having understood the basics of goal-setting using the three Ps, you can start to create your own future history. Remember 'I am the greatest!'

Once you have decided on your areas of brilliance, you can take a brave step and consider what you are holding on to in your belief system that limits you. What must you eliminate? And you can start to eliminate each limiting belief starting with the Rock.

When you get rid of the Rock, everything else becomes easier. If you have eliminated your Rock already, keep going back to your list and ask yourself, 'What else can I eliminate now? What else can I change?'

You know how to use the 'Circles of Influence versus Circles of Concern' technique. Remember the Circle of Concern is just a pity party, where you can moan and groan all you want to but it won't change anything. You now only focus your attention on your Circle of Influence.

Then we explored your values. Your values are what you build everything on. I could have started the book with values, because everything else leads from them. If your value system is right, if the belief system that you have alongside your values is pushing you in the right direction, then you'll achieve all you ever need to.

You now understand how to make those values easy to achieve. Remember who creates the rules. You do. So create simple rules, rules that are going to make a big difference to you and how you live your values.

Have you used mental rehearsal? Before you go into a meeting, before having a chat with your kids, before playing a sport? By using mental rehearsal techniques, you'll see immediately and understand the powerful difference they make.

Then it was time to create a personal vision. A vision with passion! You have explored what is important, where you want to go and how you are going to get there. You have created visual images, and you have set a timescale for taking the necessary actions. By taking those actions, within that timescale, you've joined a tiny percentage of the population who have an understanding of how to set and document their goals.

You've **created** a **personal vision!**

So now it's down to you. I know this stuff works. We know there are thousands of people who have read *How to Be Brilliant* and achieved amazing things by using the techniques you've just read. I could show you the many letters, the many emails, or let you listen to the phone calls that we get every day from people who are telling us how these techniques make a huge difference in their lives.

But that's them … What about you?

The final ingredient in your mix is to create momentum. When a rocket leaves the launch pad on a trip to the moon, it uses 95 per cent of its energy in the first three minutes. It's the initial push that is needed to break through. The same can be said of the pursuit of brilliance. The initial commitment, actions and removing of the limiting beliefs that hold you back are the keys to achieving brilliant results.

Take the great speakers Cicero and Demosthenes. After Cicero spoke, people would leap to their feet and talk about the great speech he had made. When Demosthenes spoke, they would jump to their feet and say, 'Let's march!' Are you going to be full of fine words or inspired by action?

You may also be thinking, 'I know a few people who need to change their ways to be brilliant before I can.' I agree, there are lots of people in our lives who need to change. Yet Gandhi summed it up brilliantly when he said, 'Be the change you want to see in the world.' Your actions will make a bigger difference than your knowledge.

Use these tools, apply them, step up and take action and you can have a brilliant quality of life that you could only have dreamt of.

So what happens when you do become brilliant? Easy, you learn . . .

TEN YEARS ON

I added this tiny chapter in the second edition of *How to Be Brilliant*. I don't know about you, but every now and then I like to take a few minutes to review where I am in my life and where I'd like to go next. It's the same reading a book.

What's changed in the last 10 years is that these few minutes have turned into hours, days and even weeks.

Take some time, now, for yourself (after all, you are the most important person in the world), and review where you are in your life, what's next, what you've learned and, most importantly, what actions you are going to take as a result.

12

HOW TO BE 'BRILLIANT-ER'

The next level!

So what happens once you become brilliant? Is that the end?

Actually, the path towards brilliance is a continuous and never-ending journey.

Being brilliant is a work in progress. However, having studied brilliant people (those people you and I would consider had already achieved brilliance), I've noticed something amazing. They just keep getting better.

Those who are already brilliant seem to show some interesting traits, which I think are the foundation of their continuous improvement. So rather than offering some advanced tools and techniques, I'm going to share the behaviours and attitudes that brilliant people seem to possess. It's these traits that will take you to a higher level – and keep you there.

1 Be in competition with yourself

Once you become the very best, who else is there to become better than? There's always you. In fact, even before you become the best, if you take an opportunity to beat your old self every single day, you'll improve every day. Then the only way is up.

This is particularly evident in sports. Take someone like Michael Jordan who has been described as the world's greatest ever basketball player. There is no doubt that he achieved amazing successes during his career. When he was asked who his biggest competitor was, his reply was 'Myself'.

BRILL BIT

What do you do best (or even well) and have you become a little too comfortable? It's time to be in competition with yourself and raise your game.

2 Do something totally different

Have you ever wanted to go white-water rafting or visit the most incredible places on earth? What about meeting one of your heroes or taking a risk and really finding your true self?

Often we have these conversations followed by, 'Well, if I won the lottery I would ... .' The fact is you don't have to win the lottery to experience wonderful things. Most people's goals can be achieved with dedication and commitment. Waiting for the fairy-tale lottery win is just an excuse to stay inside your comfort zone, rather than going for it and overcoming your fears and experiencing something brand new.

What are you going to do that's completely different? I've noticed that brilliant people are very open to testing out new ideas so here's a list of 10 ideas* to get your imagination started:

★ Run 10 half marathons, in 10 different countries in 10 months.

★ Hang-glide in the Alps.

★ Take up salsa dancing.

★ Visit a country a minimum of five hours away from home. Select it blindfolded with a pin.

★ Work for a charity for a month and discover your true calling.

★ Learn how to paint from a local artist.

★ Get involved with a community project and end up visiting Number 10.

★ Write a book.

★ Take up tennis – even at the age of 68.

★ Learn Italian, go to Italy to test it and meet the love of your life!

Has that inspired you to do something different? Remember, making the decision to do something is the easy part – the challenge now is to actually go out and do it.

3 Look beyond your sector

Often people become brilliant at something because it is their entire focus. They commit every waking hour and every drop of energy to get to the very top at what they do. Then once they get there they think, 'Is this it?'

If you want to go beyond brilliant, enjoy the process and feel great when you get there, take some time to look around. When you do this you'll become inspired by what's around you and, in turn, this will help you to move to your next level.

When you take the time to look outside your sector a great question to keep asking yourself is, 'How can I take these ideas, 'think transferable' and apply them into my life?'

One of my mentors has a brilliant technique for finding inspiration outside his sector. Whenever he travels, he visits the newsagents at the airport and stands in front of the magazine racks. Then he closes his eyes and moves his vision behind his eyelids. After a few moments he opens his eyes and, whichever magazine he looks at first, he buys.

*These are all ideas by readers of How to Be Brilliant who got out of their comfort zones and did something amazing!

I asked him what benefits he'd found from this. He said, 'To be honest, sometimes I find some amazing information in these magazines; other times there are only one or two things I find slightly interesting and the rest is rubbish. But I can skim pretty quickly and can dismiss the article that I won't have any use for very quickly.'

He went on to tell me about an occasion he bought a copy of the *Angling Times* – a magazine for people who are obviously interested in fishing (he's not). He struggled to find an article that was interesting. But he didn't give up and, after a short while, he did find something of interest. He explained it to me (and to be honest he had me bamboozled) but the key was this: when he adapted the seed of an idea he got from the magazine and applied it to his business, it netted him over £500,000 in less than one year. As a bonus he also managed to find a very nice rental cottage in Ireland which he and his family visit regularly, all from being a non-fisherman reading the *Angling Times*.

BRILL BIT

The secret to looking beyond your sector is to 'think transferable'. Don't limit your thinking to the first generation of what you see. Take it two or three stages forward. You'll be amazed at what you find.

There are lots of ways to look beyond your sector. Have you ever thought about doing a job swap? It may be fascinating for you to visit somebody else's place of work, for even a few hours. Once you get into the idea of looking outside what you already know, you will start to think about transferring ideas and applying those ideas in your life.

4 Find an 'Honest Joe'

An Honest Joe (or Honest Jo) is a person who will give you feedback on your performance in a ruthlessly honest way.

The chances are you probably won't have to look too far to find that person. It's probably someone who's close to you now and, if you were really honest with yourself, it's probably a person from whom you don't want to hear bad news. But once again it's a case of getting out of your comfort zone and listening to them.

Most importantly, **listen** to what they **say**

It can be difficult to listen carefully and not attempt to defend yourself when you are being given feedback that could be better. Here's a tip to help. When you receive this feedback, think about it like 'Marks & Spencer' presents. Imagine the scene. You receive a gift on your birthday from a friend or relative and you instantly know that you don't like it, but then you notice the label. It's from M&S. Hooray, it's as good as cash! You say thank you, look at it and appreciate it. Then, as soon as you can, you take it back! You don't say to them, 'Urgh! That's horrible, what makes you think I'd wear that? Are you crazy?' (Not the best way to build rapport.) It's the same with Honest Joe feedback. Even if you disagree and won't be changing a thing, you still say, 'Thank you, I appreciate your feedback,' then hold your tongue.

BRILL BIT

There are lots of unofficial Honest Joes out there who are only too happy to criticise what you do. Don't take it personally. With those people it's best to do what my friend Davina suggests, 'Ignore the critics but learn from the criticism.'

My Honest Jo is my wife, Christine. As I've made a commitment to be brilliant at presenting, she watches every appearance I make and gives me feedback at the end of it. There are times when I believe I've done a brilliant job and the feedback sheets from our clients say so. However, Christine will find a quiet moment to point out the areas where I could improve, the places where I could have been more committed or where I could have listened more carefully to the questions I was asked. She'll tell me where I could have timed things a little better and how I looked and sounded. So does it work? I've recently been described as one of the top three professional speakers in the world – that's great for my ego but it's an even stronger reason why I need an Honest Jo like Christine.

5 Become a master reframer

Studying brilliant people gives you the opportunity to see how they become the very best. One of the things I've noticed is that truly brilliant people who want to be even better are exceptionally good at reframing. I don't mean replacing the wooden surround from a picture. It's looking at situations from multiple different angles.

Here's a simple tool you can use to become a master reframer if you are in a situation where you have a conflict or you are uncomfortable with somebody. First of all, if you can physically take yourself away from the conflict area, then take a moment just to close your eyes and see the situation in multiple ways:

1 First of all through your eyes. You'll know this view – you live it.

2 Then, imagine yourself elevating above the situation and take an aerial view. What do you notice about the situation now? How do you look? How do they look?

3 Now, move into their perspective and imagine the situation from their point of view. What can they see? What do they experience? What do they notice about the situation? How do they feel?

A few years ago I used to hold one-to-one meetings with members of my team whilst sitting behind my desk. Meetings with my team were good, sometimes fantastic but rarely brilliant. I decided that if I wanted to be brilliant in this important area of discussing things with my staff, then I would need to 'reframe' the meetings.

I closed my eyes and began by looking at the meeting from my perspective, then I looked using the aerial view. Finally, I looked at the view from their perspective and the first thing I noticed was that my computer screen was just slightly to the left of where they were looking. I then framed in my mind what they would be seeing when they looked at me. I was shocked. I saw myself taking looks at the computer screen instead of being totally focused on them. A great way to disengage and appear rude. I made a conscious effort from then on that every time somebody came to my office to see me, I would step out from behind my desk and meet them in a separate area.

What can you reframe to **turn a negative into a positive**, to tidy up a mess or to just get that little bit **better**?

6 Write

As soon as you make the commitment to write about anything you know, it makes you better. It's that simple. So, if you want to be better at something, write about it. Whether it's in the form of a newsletter, a blog or even a book.

My friend, Paul Mort, decided to write an email to his database every day, sometimes twice a day. Paul's style isn't everyone's cup of tea but I've seen his writing improve and, as a result, his business has grown too. He has become better by encouraging himself to write every single day.

But what if you don't want others to read what you write? Still write. Keep a journal, write your thoughts and capture your ideas.

Writing makes you better.

7 Teach

There's a terrible expression, which you may have heard: 'Those who can, do. Those who can't, teach'. Rubbish!

How about this: 'Those who can, just go for it. Those who want to do it better, teach'.

Teaching makes you better. Whether it's coaching a colleague or coaching a friend, you naturally raise your game when you have to teach others. So, if you're already brilliant, teach others and you'll become *brilliant-er*.

It is no accident that the people who are the most brilliant continue to get even better but you don't have to wait until you feel you have brilliance as your benchmark before applying these skills. Do them now and you'll rapidly move closer towards your goal of being brilliant.

However it's not easy, life's a scrap! So what if it doesn't all go to plan? Then you'll need to know about ...

TEN YEARS ON

I've added an extra two common traits of people who just keep getting better: writing and teaching.

It's a great feeling when you know about something. And when you can share that knowledge with others, it feels even better.

Ten years ago I had a much stronger impulse to hold on to my ideas. They were mine and I wanted to keep them. Crazy when I think that my big goal in life was to positively influence a million lives! Even crazier as most of 'my' ideas were inspired by others. There are very few original ideas in personal development.

And if you thought that the evolution of the internet was encouraging more people to share their ideas, you'll be surprised to learn that, while 95 per cent of people use the internet to gain knowledge, only 5 per cent add to it. Go on – post a blog, share an idea, contribute.

These days I share my ideas with as many people as possible. Even if they are my competitors, that's fine, because over the last 10 years I've realized something: the more knowledge I share, the more knowledge I get back.

So if you'd like to be brilliant-er, then learning more is a great start. But if you focus on sharing more, that's what will make the biggest difference.

13

OVERCOMING OBSTACLES
What stops brilliance?

Since *How to Be Brilliant* was first published, I have been contacted by many readers who had applied the tools and techniques from the book, and found their lives transformed. Not only did they find that they had increased wealth, health, work success, better relationships etc. but they also found brilliance in other areas of their lives. However, we also found there was a significant group of people who, just as soon as they got started with their *How to Be Brilliant* tools and techniques, found they were facing setbacks.

If you don't know how to address these setbacks properly, it is very easy to stumble and fall during your first 90 days of massive action. Here are the top five most common setbacks and how you can overcome them.

1 Procrastination

Even though, throughout this book, I suggest readers take action now and do the exercises straight away, I still find that a significant number of people read the book first and 'say' they are going to take the actions but they never do.

Now *How to Be Brilliant* includes a simple checklist to ensure you have carried out all the exercises. You can find it on page 158. If you are unable to do an exercise as you read, you can use the checklist to make sure you catch up with every one later. If you've missed any, you can schedule a time when you will complete them.

This is very important and will really help you to become brilliant by creating momentum. When you create momentum it's much easier to keep going. Keep this list in a highly visible place and it will stir you into action.

> **BRILL BIT**
>
> If you want to overcome procrastination in any area, keep your next actions visible.
>
> I love this tip: if you want to take more exercise, keep your training shoes next to the front door – you'll run more often!
>
> **Remember – the secret isn't in the knowing, the secret is in the doing.**

2 Other people

Wouldn't it be great if you were surrounded by fabulous, supportive people who really wanted you to be brilliant in all the key areas of your life? And these people gave you enough time, freedom and the opportunity to do everything that you've read in this book?

The reality is that some will but many won't. You will become most like the people you spend most of your time with. Think about who those people are right now. It may be that you are surrounded by very inspirational people who will stretch and encourage you. However, you may be surrounded by some people who just do not subscribe to what you've been learning and actively work to prevent your progress. Then you have a very simple choice.

We used to run a course for young people called 'Beyond Brilliant'. During the programme, often with teenagers, we looked at who they chose to spend their time with. Sometimes it becomes blatantly obvious to these young people the reasons why they are not achieving everything they want in their lives. The top reason? The people who they are spending their time with are not supportive and they are being dragged down. We then gave them this piece of advice:

You can either *lead your group* or

leave your group

If you choose to lead your group then you have to take on responsibilities as a leader and continue to move up to the next level, regardless of what other people think. If you don't think you can do this then maybe it's time to spend less time with the people who are holding you back.

Can you change other people? Yes, but …

At the end of our presentations, one of the most common questions I am asked is: 'If I decide to be brilliant, what can I do about the people around me? What if they don't want to change?' I refer them back to that wonderful quote by Gandhi: 'Be the change you want to see in the world.' In other words, stop spending time wanting to change other people and just focus on being brilliant yourself first.

It's amazing that when people see what you're doing and the difference you're making in your life they'll be quick to ask you how you're doing it.

3 Levels of energy

How would you feel if I suggested that you got out of bed an hour earlier every day and spent 60 minutes working on how to be brilliant? I guess if you are like most people that prospect is terrifying. The chances are high that you are one of the millions of people who wake up tired every day.

Low levels of energy, whether it be when you wake up, throughout the day or when you need some oomph, are one of the biggest factors that stop people from being brilliant.

There are some things you can do to increase your energy levels very quickly so that you can be your best, feel full of energy throughout the day, work hard into the night and have the energy to get up early and feel refreshed. I'm 90 per cent sure you'll know these already but it's worthwhile reminding yourself of them.

It's also worthwhile remembering that knowing them isn't really enough, it's the ... (fill in the space!):

★ **Take exercise.** Exercise gives you energy. Not only that, it enables you to live longer, feel healthier and rejuvenates your often tired body.

★ **Drink lots of water.** By staying hydrated, your body works better. Pure water is the number-one fuel for your body, so drink plenty.

★ **Eat the right stuff.** I could just end this paragraph here because through the education that we've had, especially in the past few years, you know the right stuff to eat. Brilliant people are eating the right stuff every day.

★ **Look after your body before you get a health problem.** Take regular massages, visit an osteopath or chiropractor and have some treatments. Look after the most important person in the world first – that's you!

★ **Create a positive attitude that supports your healthy, energetic body.** By telling yourself you're tired, you have no energy or you feel ill, you'll become what you focus on. Start to tell yourself that you are the picture of health and that you have huge amounts of energy. You will find your natural energy lasting throughout the day.

4 Lack of resources

I'm always surprised when people say that they don't have the resources that they need.

BRILL BIT

It's not the lack of resources but the lack of resourcefulness that most people suffer from.

If you really want to find the resource to do what you need to do, then you will find it. It's out there but you have to look harder, ask better questions and be more active. You have to make it a must.

The most common resource that people believe they lack is money. But this needn't be the case if you have the right attitude towards receiving money and take the correct actions towards achieving it.

Simon Woodroffe, the founder of YO! Sushi and YOtel, told me how when he needed money to start YO! Sushi he was inspired by reading Goethe: 'When you are truly committed the world conspires to help you in all sorts of ways you could never believe possible including the provision of financial assistance.' The part he really liked was the last few words.

If that's the case – and I believe it is – then you can create the resource that you need, be it financial, time, information, physical or mental. You just need a burning desire first, then a commitment to see it through.

5 Setbacks that are outside your control

If you believe, as I do, that everything happens for a reason then you can always look at setbacks as an opportunity to learn. Now that last sentence was easy to write, easy to read but very challenging to do.

Sometimes you'll wonder 'What is the lesson?' But usually, through time and reflection, you understand that what you saw as 'setbacks' are actually some of the most valuable life lessons.

BRILL BIT

Life lessons can come in disguise, so unmasking the lesson is the key. Ask yourself this question: 'What have learned?'

My uncle used to say, 'If it doesn't kill you, it'll make you stronger.' As a young person I never quite knew what this meant but I think I'm starting to understand it now. The positive person I am today has grown more through dealing with the difficult times than enjoying the good times.

> *'Enjoy when times are good and accept when times are not.'*
> (SIMON WOODROFFE)

Your journey towards being brilliant is going to feature some setbacks, lack of time, procrastination, other people's beliefs, low energy levels and at times an apparent lack of resources.

Guess what – you're no different from anybody else who has travelled on this journey before you. All you can do is take solace in the knowledge that, at the end of the day, it is worth it. Thousands of people have benefited from *How to Be Brilliant*: you can be inspired by what they have done, but most of all you can learn from their ...

When I initially wrote *How to Be Brilliant,* the closest thing we had to social media was Friends Reunited. Do you remember? You'd check in a couple of times a week and see who else from your old school or workplace had joined.

Now social media is integrated into every part of life. For some, the first thing to do each morning when they wake is to log on to Twitter or Facebook to see what's happened overnight. It's a challenge for some folk to have a night out and to be 'in the moment' without the need to upload a 'selfie' to Instagram or to check in with Foursquare.

Please don't think I'm anti social media, but you do have to ask, 'Is this helping me to be better? Is it helping me to be brilliant?'

A friend of mine shared a liberating story from her daughter, who decided to delete her Instagram account. She did it because of the pressures of, 'Always having to look good', 'Documenting everything' and 'Worrying about the comments: who left them, who didn't and why'. She told her mum that she didn't want to look back on her childhood and her memories be based around what did or didn't happen on Instagram.

So while attempting to be more connected with people, be careful you don't become more detached from life.

Another obstacle to overcome is the sheer volume of information and opportunity that comes our way. What hasn't changed is that we still have the exact same amount of time to fit everything in.

Learning how to say 'No', and to say it nicely, is a real key in the world we live in now. But we worry. What if we say 'No' and miss out on an opportunity or upset someone? What if we don't get that opportunity ever again?

If you have those thoughts, then now may be a good time to revisit Chapter 5 – 'Brilliant belief systems', and create a new belief. It's OK to say 'No'.

14

BRILLIANT LIFE LESSONS

You could probably write your own book, or at least a chapter, on the life lessons you've picked up over the years: from the big 'If it doesn't kill you, it'll make you stronger' moments to the things that seemed insignificant at the time but lead to amazing changes in your life. It's worth reflecting on these, as it makes you more conscious of them and, as new life lessons come along, you'll be more aware of them occurring at the time.

Here is a quick summary of the most valuable life lessons I've learned – the events or moments that changed my life and by a strange and fortuitous route got me to where I am today.

I'm always keen to hear about the life lessons of others, as it's a fabulous way of learning. It's amazing how others' lessons can change your thinking about your own life. I hope the following will help you think differently.

Like you, I've had dozens of life lessons, but some have had a bigger impact than others. The first big one came when I left school aged 16 and immediately started to work in my father's business as an apprentice roofer. I always knew I wanted to be a roofer right from the age of 9 when my Dad said to me, 'Son, one day this will all be yours.' At 9 years old the prospect of owning two vans and six ladders is quite exciting!

However about a week after I started and faced the humiliation from the other lads of being 'the boss's son', I realized that roofing wasn't for me and I made a decision to leave. Seven years later I built up the courage to actually tell my Dad that I was never destined to be in a conventional business and I had found a new job. He was thrilled for me! I discovered that no matter what, he wanted me to be happy. That day I learned ...

Valuable life lesson number 1

If you don't love it don't do it.

I don't mean you have to love every minute of every day but what I am saying to you is if you are reading this book and have a job you hate then find a way to love it or find a way to leave it. You are at work half of your waking hours! A third of your life!

Don't get me wrong, my time wasn't wasted. My father taught me a huge amount about values. He would never take an easier route to make a quick profit: he would commit to spending hours with apprentices to teach them the highest quality craftsmanship and give unconditionally of his time and resources to ensure that something was right. He trained the British roofing team, who went on to win the world championships (I bet you never knew there was a roofing world championship!) and helped hundreds of people around the world. This was my first experience of brilliance.

I left to work for a youth organization. I'd been a volunteer for many years but this was an offer to be paid to do something I enjoyed doing for free! I was offered a job by a brilliant man called Allan Percival. Where other people saw a daft roofer who liked to muck about, 'Percy' saw something more and gave me a chance. A chance that completely changed my life.

Valuable life lesson number 2

You'll meet people who want to help you and give you a chance. Let them.

From working as a professional youth worker I ended up managing a large project with lots of different charities at the National Garden Festival 1990 in Gateshead. I had the job of ensuring the charities had everything they needed to be successful at the event. It wasn't long before I realized some charities were going to raise a lot more than others. In fact, looking at the figures each week, I noticed that 20 per cent of the charities were raising 80 per cent of the money and the other 80 per cent were fighting over the remaining 20 per cent. One organization in particular stood out: the Northumberland Wildlife Trust. Its staff seemed to do everything better than most, but on closer inspection I discovered they had some interesting characteristics. They arrived early, left late, worked harder and connected with more people than any other organization. Did they raise more money? You bet they did! Day after day, week after week. I was puzzled. Why didn't others spot what they were doing and remodel their strategies accordingly? It's only now that I truly understand why and it was the key to their success which has remained with me for life: their team was brilliant!

Valuable life lesson number 3

Brilliance does not happen by accident. It's about planning, hard work and skill.

I eventually became a fundraiser myself for a charity that became the most successful ever in the North of England. Looking back, I now know that some of the techniques I was applying were great personal development tools. The only way we could be so successful was by having a great attitude, by being able to set new standards, and by breaking out of limiting beliefs that would hold many other people back.

My next job was working with another charity but this time I was responsible for bringing in large donations. One day I had the privilege of meeting David

Brown. He's the chap who invented the gearing mechanism for the Caterpillar, the large, split-axle truck that you'll see in quarries throughout the world. David Brown was a very gentle man but completely focused. After a long conversation with him (with me asking most of the questions about his life, and what he had achieved), he turned to me and said, 'Michael, what are you doing about your own personal development?' I didn't really understand the question, so I asked him to be more specific. He asked me about the books I read, the courses I'd been on (ones that I paid for!). My answers were mumbled and muddled. I wasn't doing anything about my personal development. My life was passing me by. So after some soul searching, I knew the time had come for me to take some positive action.

I started to read personal development books. The first one was called *Think and Grow Rich* by Napoleon Hill. I have since read that book over 20 times. The next book was *How to Win Friends and Influence People* by Dale Carnegie. Two classics. I realized that if I wanted to improve myself (and others) I had to get additional knowledge. To get that information I devoted myself to consistent and never-ending improvement. I made a commitment to read a book a week and did so for two years. That is one of the reasons why I thank you for reading this book because reading can be a challenge in our busy lives.

When I was reading a book a week, I was also listening to as many audio recordings from as many different authors and experts as I could. I booked myself on to personal development courses because I knew that if I wanted to improve, I had to invest in my own future. Much of this book is influenced by many of those early books I read, the audio I listened to and the courses I attended.

Valuable life lesson number 4

Read, read and read! Become a glutton for knowledge. You can learn a person's life's work from one book. When applied, every penny and every second you invest in your learning will pay back at a rate you could only have dreamed of.

It was during a personal development training programme that I realized my destiny was to present this type of material. Shortly afterwards I was given the opportunity to teach a course to children at weekends. The course achieved amazing results. In fact, kids were going back to school and their teachers were asking, 'Wow, what happened to you?' Not only were they academically better but their social skills had improved, their confidence levels soared, even their sport was enhanced. In fact there was an all-round improvement.

Teachers started to come to see our courses and began to understand what we were doing. It wasn't long before there was a lot of interest from educational bodies. I was given the opportunity to teach teachers the skills and techniques that we were using in our programme.

The day I walked through the school gates to teach teachers for the first time was the day I realized that teaching teachers is tough! That may surprise you but I learned quickly. I stood up in front of this group of teachers and began explaining passionately many different ideas and how they could possibly work in their school. The teachers were not engaged at all! They sat with their arms folded, heads to one side with their eyes rolled back. I asked myself, 'What's wrong with these people, why don't they understand – why is it that they won't take these ideas and use them right now?'

After 45 minutes I needed to change things. A few weeks beforehand I had been on a presentation skills course. The leader of the programme gave this advice, 'If you should ever feel like you are losing an audience simply ask if anyone has any questions or comments. No one will put their hands up and then you can move on, showing your audience that you are in control.' It turned out that that was the single worst piece of advice I had ever heard!

'Does anyone have any questions or comments?' I asked. Can you imagine my surprise when about 50 hands shot up! I panicked and tried to pick someone whom I thought looked 'weak'. I scanned the hall and noticed there was a very old lady sitting in the back row, I thought she looked nice and safe. 'Yes the lady at the back, what's your question?'

It was at that exact moment that I learned ...

Valuable life lesson number 5

Appearances can be deceptive!

It turns out the very old lady had been teaching in a tough secondary school for over 30 years! My advice now is never to judge people by age, gender, size, shape, looks, title or anything else before you even know them.

She asked three questions in rapid succession.

1 'Whose research is this based on?'

2 'Where are the scientific facts to back up your ideas?'

3 'What's the cognitive process that takes place in the neo-cortex when the brain processes positive language?'

To be honest she'd lost me after, 'What's the ...'. Have you ever had that sick feeling in your stomach which at the time you think will never go away? For the rest of the day those teachers gave me the hardest training experience of my life.

I realized it was all very well knowing that these ideas worked, but how was I going to get the supporting scientific evidence?

Do you believe the right people appear at the right time in your life? I do. With a head full of questions, I met a great man called Professor John MacBeath OBE. At that time he was Head of Quality in Education at the University of Strathclyde, Glasgow. He moved on to be Professor Emeritus of Leadership in the Faculty of Education at Cambridge University. Here's a man who really knows his stuff, and he offered to help me with my work in education. We have become very close friends because he was able to demonstrate not only how the ideas worked, but also *why* they worked. Once we added to this the research to back up the ideas, we had a winning combination. I was so excited. Once again I was in a learning curve, a huge accelerated learning curve! This time we could touch the lives of many millions of young people through working in education.

Valuable life lesson number 6

The right people turn up at the right time.

So keep your eyes open. You never know, the person sitting opposite you on the train, or that friend of a friend could hold the answer to so many questions in your life. But if you don't talk to them, you'll never know.

Within the space of a few months, we moved from school halls to the World Thinking Conference in Singapore, and had the privilege of presenting our work to an international audience of people from 52 countries. We were able to demonstrate different ideas and techniques that were really working in education. Our model is now used in many countries throughout the world, and I am very proud to have been a part of it. I also realized in Singapore it was time to do something for *me* .... . So, 90 days later I'd resigned from my job, moved house, written a new series of training sessions, reset all my personal goals and started my own organization, Michael Heppell Limited, with a vision to positively influence one million lives.

Starting my own business would create the biggest highs and deepest lows in my life. My first challenge was that when I started very few people (in fact, thinking back, it was nobody) wanted to listen to me and my ideas on how I could help them.

After a disastrous first year, with no money, no clients, no office and terrible family strains I became desperate and took on anything that came my way. This included selling cheap telephone calls, event management, designing newsletters and a range of open programmes that were mainly attended by family, friends and the occasional paying client. After a year of this crazy behaviour the biggest blow of all occurred when my wife left me and took our kids.

I'd learned another very costly lesson.

Valuable life lesson number 7

Being busy does not mean you are being successful.

This was compounded by the big one ...

Valuable life lesson number 8

Your family ARE more important than your career.

The next few years mainly featured a millennium, a new focused Michael and a couple of people who not only gave me the chance to work with their organizations, but who also told lots of others about the successes we had.

I created a programme called 'How to Be Brilliant'. It began as a two-day event which included 25 hours of presentation time! I loved it but the participants were leaving with brain overload and an overwhelming sense of too much to do. It was around that time I learned ...

Valuable life lesson number 9

You don't have to teach people everything you know – at least not all of it in the first 48 hours.

My organization started to grow and, more importantly, I sorted myself out by focusing on what was really important. Best of all, Christine and I remarried! Then, just when I thought life couldn't get any better, Rachael Stock, the best publisher in the world, gave me the opportunity to write a book.

I had no idea at that time how successful I could be as an author or if anyone would want to buy a book written by me. I didn't know if I could write. In fact my English teacher wrote on my final school report, 'Michael will never do anything with the English language.' I didn't really have the time. I have a form of dyslexia that means I jumble up and reverse words. And I knew I didn't have the talent. With all that in mind, and a crazy deadline to hit, there was one big question – what should it be called?' 'What about *How to Be Brilliant?*' she suggested.

And that's ...

Valuable life lesson number 10

Even when there's a dozen reasons why not, sometimes you just have to go for it anyway.

I hope you've enjoyed the results so far. I hope you've found some inspiration, not from what I've done (I'm just a very normal guy) but from the life lessons that I've drawn out from my story. These are lessons that millions of other people have learned too – often the hard way.

Now if you really want to be inspired by what others have done then I've one more chapter for you. I asked people to share their brilliant stories and quickly found there are some inspirational people who have done really amazing things. So read on and you too will feel inspired with ...

TEN YEARS ON

Deciding what to focus on

My kids like to take the mickey out of me because I've been known to say, 'I've reached that point in my life when, if I don't want to do something, I don't have to'. I'm 47. There's a brilliant life lesson: not so much the 'not doing what you don't want to do', but focusing on the stuff you really do want to do.

In the last 10 years I've learned that many of the things you consider important now won't mean anything in 10 years' time. Of course, the flip side of that is also true.

Making values-based decisions makes decision-making easier; never easy, just easier.

Add value

A business life lesson I've learned over the last 10 years is the importance of maintaining your price and your principles. The global economic crisis has had a massive impact on many businesses. Cutting costs, then quality, then desperately cutting your price to gain a competitive edge became an all too familiar cycle.

Christine (my wife and business partner) insisted we wouldn't cut our fees. A race to the bottom wasn't what we taught, and it certainly wouldn't be what we would do. Instead, we would add even more value. Our team worked tirelessly to secure every event and I worked harder than ever to perfect my craft as a speaker and trainer.

There were plenty of times when this approach could have been a lot easier. The temptation to drop our fees or spend less time preparing was ever present. When times were really tough, we heard from other professional speakers who were slashing their prices to grab any business that was available. Even 'celebrity' speakers were halving their fees. But the life lesson we learned was simple – our clients wanted quality and value, more than discounts.

There will be another recession, there will be more tough times, and when they do come, think carefully. Before you reduce your fees or close shop, could you add more value first?

BRILLIANCE UNCOVERED

One of the wonderful things about creating revised editions of a book is the opportunity to share with new readers a few of the things that happened to some of the many tens of thousands of earlier readers. I know you aren't necessarily interested in the intricacies of the lives of random strangers – be reassured, this chapter is still about you. It's all about reading, thinking, understanding and applying the lessons to your own life.

The key to getting the most out of this short chapter is to *think transferable*. If you read a story and don't think it applies to you because you're older than that, or it's not in your sector, then you'll have missed a trick. Enjoy the power of these stories, feel inspired and take action.

Brilliant families

So how do you get your family to sit down, share their challenges and aspirations and spend some quality time together? That's what the Lee family in Singapore wanted, and the Wheel of Life was the answer.

Mum had bought *How to Be Brilliant* because she liked the cover (as good a reason as any) but once she started to read she became fascinated with the Wheel of Life and its many applications. After completing her wheel for the first time, she decided the whole family should do theirs. She downloaded copies for everyone from **www.michaelheppell.com** and set herself a short-term goal to persuade her whole family (five of them) to complete their wheels together. She changed *work* for *education* for her teenage sons and made this family event a must for everyone.

Two days later they had finished their evening meal and set about the task of completing their wheels. Each area on the wheel was discussed. Because Mum and Dad were open and honest it wasn't long before the whole Lee family were sharing their hopes and dreams and analysing the Rocks that were holding them back. They were able to support and help each other work towards a balanced wheel.

Brilliant guidance

Jane used to get completely overwhelmed with challenges. This heightened anxiety was something she would try to hide but the people closest to her could 'feel something wasn't right'. She decided to use the Mastermind Group idea from Chapter 6 to see how others would deal with the challenges she faced.

'Things that seemed hard to deal with appear simple and straightforward within my advisor's eyes,' she said. And she was right. By getting a different perspective on a challenge you often see that the problem isn't so big, or you work out a way and soon find the solution.

Brilliance in education

I've worked a lot in education. I used to joke that teachers were the hardest people on the planet to actually teach! After 20 years teaching teachers I now know it's no joke – it's true. The reality is, it's never been harder for teachers. Higher expectations from parents, government and stakeholders make the actual job of teaching an ever-increasing challenge. And the brilliant news is that in almost every school and college where we work these special people are rising to the challenge. And none more so than in Freebrough Community College.

Freebrough would be the first to admit they have some challenges, but they also have a firm belief that, no matter what is thrown at them, they'll overcome it.

They used *How to Be Brilliant* at many levels. First, the Senior Team made a commitment to raise their benchmark to brilliance. They did this when they were several months behind on a new building programme, two schools were about to be merged into one and they had gone through a very difficult inspection. This is a time when many other people would have 'put it off' until things calmed down – the fact is, in education these days, it will never calm down.

Then they involved all their staff – everyone – from Heads of Department to cleaning staff and, because they really wanted everyone to know their ambition, they arranged a separate event for local businesses and stake-holders and I was their guest speaker. They told the group with such passion about their goal to be brilliant that they got 100 per cent support and funding from several of the businesses to help finance their vision.

Then they took every pupil on a 'Brilliance into action' experience. This included 90 days of a massive action campaign, which included preparation for exams, improving behaviour and building confidence.

The results have been incredible. As I write this I have just revisited the school as the guest speaker at their Annual Awards Evening. Everyone I talked to had a success story – some big, some small, but all brilliant.

Who could you take with you on your journey to brilliance?

Brilliance in a small business

When Matt, the MD of a recruitment company, saw *How to Be Brilliant* in London's King's Cross Station he bought it to read on the train journey back to his office in Leeds. During that short trip, not only did he read the book (a record?) but he also made a commitment that the recruitment company he had started with his wife four years previously was going to be brilliant.

Matt bought copies for all of his team and held regular West Wing meetings with only one agenda item, 'How to Be Brilliant'. They had dozens of great ideas, from their vision 'To be recognized as the most hospitable recruitment company in the world' to their now legendary '5 o'clock Chablis' events, where they invite clients to visit their office on a Friday afternoon to share their success.

Creativity shone from the team, a perfect example being in their brilliant use of language:

Wouldn't you love your company to have a staff **recognition** scheme where the **prizes** are kept in the 'rewardrobe'?

Brilliance in the public sector

One of the biggest challenges of working in a large public-sector organization is the feeling that you are a small cog in a very large machine. Sally felt that way and here's what she wrote:

> 'I must say, when Carole, my boss, gave me *How to Be Brilliant* I was very sceptical. So it did surprise me that it was very much a book for me personally. I thought it was going to be about being brilliant in my job, but it was much more about being brilliant in myself – for me!
>
> 'The key moment for me came when I realized that how I felt about my work was up to me. I used the Circles of Influence versus Circles of Concern to assess what I could do to make my job more rewarding. It really worked.
>
> 'Best of all I started to reply, "Brilliant" whenever anyone asked me how I was. The look on people's faces was priceless!'

Brilliance in sport

Recently I have been asked to work in the wonderful world of professional football. As a person who could have been a lot better at football at school I can't help but smile as I help Premiership players to build their careers, or national teams to prepare for international duty.

One of the key messages I find top sports people take from *How to Be Brilliant* is the understanding of brilliant belief systems. I can't help them with their tactics or physical skills but I can help them achieve rapid change and improvement with their mental game.

So, if you play a sport, ask yourself, 'What is your belief system when you go out and play?' Do you go for it and give 100 per cent all the time or do you hold back in case your going for 100 per cent causes failure? When you walk out ready for the game, do you see yourself as the most feared player or do you fear the opposition?

The **mental** game is what takes players from **fantastic** to brilliant

Brilliant relationships

Here's the letter just as I received it from Tony.

Dear Michael

Thank you for *How to Be Brilliant* – it has saved my marriage and possibly my life. Let me tell you how so you can hopefully share this with others.

I bought *How to Be Brilliant* because I wanted to be better at what I spend most of my time doing now, working hard with my business partner in a new venture (two years old). The weird thing was, as I read the chapter on values I made a shattering discovery. My values and my wonderful wife's were miles apart. I almost ignored it and hoped things would 'just get better' but I couldn't get the words 'Massive action = massive results' out of my head. I ran straight upstairs and shared what I discovered with my wife.

Three hours later, in the early hours of the morning, we had completed the 'Life Question' and 'Values' exercises together and for the first time I realized that I had no idea what my wife's true values were. I know what I thought they were, I know what I thought they should be, but I had no idea what they really were.

Now we are aligned and we've made some easy rules to help us to experience our core values more often. I'm more understanding, she's more tolerant and life's … brilliant!

Thank you

Tony

Brilliant financials

Gavin is 56 and he's spent his whole life 'just getting by'. He's never saved more than £500 in his life and he thought he never would. Gavin read *How to Be Brilliant* and, by the time he is 60, he will be worth a small fortune.

At first, after reading *How to Be Brilliant*, Gavin did nothing. He didn't do the exercises and he didn't have a 90-day massive action plan. Six months later he was made redundant when the company where he had worked for 15 years closed. That's when he picked up *How to Be Brilliant* for the second time.

This time Gavin noticed (in his words), 'I had all those characteristics you wrote about. The only thing I didn't have was a mindset that I should be doing it for me.' Gavin started his own company and, with the help of some great friends, is set to double his expected profits for the next five years. His advice? 'Don't wait until you have to do something because someone else is in control. Be yourself and you will be surprised at what you can achieve.'

Brilliant work

Nigel was working as a sign-writer when he read *How to Be Brilliant,* but that wasn't where he wanted to be in his heart. He wanted to tour the world and, more than that, he wanted to share with people his excitement and passion for travel.

Within a year Nigel had reinvented himself as a travel guide. Brilliant!

Many people have changed jobs and are now doing the job they love because of a kick-start with *How to Be Brilliant*. Craig left the world of factory flooring to become a football agent, Jennifer left HR to become an author and there are hundreds of others who have shared their stories with us. What I loved about Nigel was how he describes his relationship with *How to Be Brilliant* now, 'I use it like a tool bag in the form of a diary. It gives me that help when my direction gets a little lost.'

Brilliant leverage

When Jayne confessed to being a hoarder and having a house full of junk, which she could 'never get round to throwing out', it took the guts of the trainer (me) on her time management programme to come up with a brilliant solution. I asked for her address, asked how many bags of junk and rubbish she thought she could fill, and in front of the rest of the group called the local authority and arranged for 40 bags of rubbish to be collected three weeks later. Jayne got over the initial shock and suddenly realized that it was time to take action. Within a week she had filled the 40 bags and went on to fill a further 20 with rubbish and a further 30 for charity shops! Ninety bags of junk had filled her life. It's amazing what you'll do for a man in a van!

I could write another book based on the successes of people who have used *How to Be Brilliant* but, at the end of the day, this book was written for one person only, and that's you.

I hope I have challenged you to have brilliance as your benchmark and to start with 90 days of massive action. Now that you know it – the secret is to do it. So go on, be brilliant!

What did you think of this book?

We're really keen to hear from you about this book, so that we can make our publishing even better.

Please log on to the following website and leave us your feedback.

It will only take a few minutes and your thoughts are invaluable to us.

www.pearsoned.co.uk/bookfeedback

HOW TO BE BRILLIANT EXERCISE CHECKLIST

How have you done? Take a look at the list below and ask yourself, 'As I read this book did I do it or do I just know it?' Remember: *the secret isn't in the knowing, it's in the doing.*

So ensure you have completed and ticked off all the tasks below and you'll be well on the road to brilliance!

1   Completed your Wheel of Life.

2   Started the bonus 30-day challenge to change your language.

3   Began conversations with five strangers in 24 hours.

4   Learned to relax.

5   Written long-term goals: 90 days; 1, 5 and 10 years using the three Ps.

6   Created your written commitment to being brilliant.

7   Listed everything that holds you back and identified your Rock.

8   Reframed your language based around your Rock.

9   Completed Circles of Influence versus Circles of Concern.

10 Found a mentor.

| 11 | Created a Mastermind Group. | ▦ |

11   Created a Mastermind Group. ▦

12   Identified your Life Question. ▦

13   Rewritten your Life Question. ▦

14   Identified your current values and put them in order. ▦

15   Written down the description of the person you ultimately
     want to become. ▦

16   Rewritten your values and put them in order. ▦

17   Created the rules for your new values and created a
     visual image of them. ▦

18   Your brilliant vision checklist:

     ★ Selected visual images. ▦

     ★ Created a vision book. ▦

     ★ Written the three Ps affirmations. ▦

     ★ Noted dates they will be achieved by. ▦

     ★ Created a list of resources and people who can help. ▦

     ★ Written 30-, 7- and 1-day massive action plans. ▦

19   Registered with **www.michaelheppell.com** and asked for
     the free bonus chapter. ▦

APPENDIX

Michael Heppell Ltd company values

Brilliance

We are brilliant in all our actions, we 'step up' and go the extra mile towards achieving our goals.

Integrity

We tell the truth and focus on delivering correct information and feed back to each other and our clients.

Positive belief

We use positive language, tackle challenges in a positive way and choose to see a positive side of every given situation. We understand that we create our own belief systems based on the evidence we search for, so we choose to create positive empowering belief systems.

Shared goals

We share our goals with each other and make a commitment to help each other achieve those goals. We understand that by sharing goals we do so in confidence.

Second mile and surprise

We continuously go the second mile and surpass our clients' expectations. We, when appropriate, create pleasant surprises for our clients.

Family first

We believe that our families will come first. This means that it is expected we support our families and communicate when we are doing this to our colleagues and, if necessary, clients.

Fun!

We create a genuine, fun atmosphere in our work and we create a place where we can express ourselves in creative and supportive surroundings. We give our clients fun experiences. We ensure our fun experiences are not at the expense of others.

Best value

We provide best value for our clients and if requested give detailed break-downs of any costs incurred. We expect best value from our suppliers and business partners and search for this when we engage them with our company.

Team respect and communication

We respect each other and work together for a common goal. We communicate respectfully with one another. We do what we say we will do. We turn up on time and work until the job is done. We communicate with each other when challenges arise and seek first to understand.

Learning

We are committed to lifelong learning and actively encourage an environment where learning can take place.

THANK YOU TO ...

Bill & Liz Heppell for Brilliant parenting
Andrew Heppell for Brilliant big brothering
Lea McConnell for being a Brilliant best school friend
Gav, Nonk, Sav, Cookie, Sev, Nessy & Carolyn for Brilliant teens
Tommy & Nora Cartmell for a Brilliant love of youth
The Revd Barrie Lees for Brilliant guidance
Uncle Donald, Aunty Elaine & family for Brilliant summers
Aunty Ethel and Uncle Alan for Brilliantly remembering
The Officers & volunteers of the Boys' Brigade for Brilliant youth work
Jimmy Severs for being ruddy Brilliant
Kevin O'Neil for Brilliant teaching
Janice Smith for Brilliant big teas
Paul Raisbeck for being a Brilliant roadie, still
Lisa Raisbeck for Brilliant rabbit feeding
Edgar & Nug for a Brilliant band
All my colleagues for Brilliant work times
Allan Percival for seeing Brilliance
Newcastle Magic Circle for Brilliant dexterity
Gary Smith for Brilliant events
Darren Sowerby for Brilliant technology
David Grant for Brilliant belief
Claire Hayhurst for being the Brilliant iron woman
Sir Paul Nicholson for Brilliant vision
David Brown for a Brilliant challenge
Belinda Jayne Sloan for the Brilliant Common Purpose
Prof. John MacBeath for the most Brilliant mind
Richard Watts for Brilliant trimming
Jill Telfer for Brilliant godmothering
Jack & Norma Black for a Brilliant life lesson
Cliff Walker for a Brilliant opportunity
Steve & Yvette Mitchell for Brilliant fun in the sun
Ian Smith for Brilliant team building

Justine Hayhurst for Brilliantly being there
Chris Hampton for Brilliant fun
Jo Walker for Brilliant fingers
Dr Fiona Ellis for Brilliant osteopathy
Ray Cranston for Brilliant 'slippas'
Jeffrey Gitomer for Brilliant sales training
James Pink for Brilliant humour
Wil Cheung for Brilliant hospitality
Martin Warden & Hi Lights for Brilliant sound and light
All at the Design Group (DECIDE.) Newcastle for Brilliant creativity
David Miller for Brilliant bacon and stilton baps and total faith
Sir David Bell for a Brilliant introduction
Dave Thorp for Brilliant film making
The Lamb family for being Brilliant neighbours
Robert Savage for Brilliant Bondi experiences
Stephen Deakin for a Brilliant introduction to five-star service
Mo Hanslod for Brilliant persistence
The locals at The Hadrian in Wall for Brilliant nights out
Doreen Soulsby for being a Brilliant first PA
Jeremy Taylor for Brilliant chairmanship with friendship
Stevie Pattison-Dick for Brilliantly telling everyone
Joan & Martin Fisher for Brilliant 'housekeeping and maintenance'
Carrot Media for Brilliantly demystifying the web
Red Carnation Hotels our Brilliant home from home
Stephanie Chiswell for Brilliantly always finding a room
Dawson & Sanderson for Brilliant travel
Peter Field for being a Brilliant coach
Glyn Davies for being a Brilliant student
Sarah Scott for Brilliantly diving in to help
Irene Dorner for Brilliantly showing how business and friendship works
Simon Woodroffe for being BrilliYOnt
Fat Tony for Brilliantly mixing up life
Suze & KT for Brilliant TV mentoring
Philip Ball for the Brilliant soundtracks to my life
Steve Walker for Brilliant faith that we'd do it
Richard Nugent for Brilliant lads lunches
Vanessa Thompson for Brilliantly being the world's greatest PA
Sheila Storey for Brilliant number crunching
Ruth Thomson for Brilliant business generation
Alastair Walker for Brilliant communication
Norman & Neil at KCS Datawright for Brilliantly fixing everything IT
Malcolm Kyle for being a Brilliant networker
Michael Foster & The Rights House for being my Brilliant agent

Annabel Merullo for doing Brilliant book deals
Matthew and Davina Robertson for Brilliantly 'sharing the love'
Jonathan & Penny Raggett for being our Brilliant London pals
Tim Brownson for being the Brilliant no BS coach
Liz and Paul McGowan for a Brilliant welcome
Simon Perkins for Brilliantly being the most fun client
Patrick Kielty for your Brilliant intellect
John Kennedy for Brilliantly getting us there on time, every time
Gilly Thirlwell for Brilliantly teaching us yoga
Jazz FM for a ba bap ba-rilliant background
Jack Krellé for Brilliantly challenging the thinking
Eloise Cook for a Brilliant tenth edition
All the Michael Heppell staff, past and future, for making it 'a Brilliant day'
Everyone at Pearson for Brilliant publishing
Paul East for Brilliantly pushing
Rachael Stock for being my Brilliant publisher and friend

You for Brilliantly reading this far

To everyone else who has touched my life, you know who you are, thank you for being Brilliant

And God for every Brilliant thing

INDEX

30-day challenges 15–16, 18–19
90-day massive action plan xvi,
    43–7, 118–20

action
    asking for help 86–7
    mental rehearsal 42–3, 115–18
    positive action 14–20
    selecting areas for brilliance 58–9
    see also massive action;
      procrastination
adrenalin 29–30
affirmations 72–4, 109, 113
age 73
Ali, Muhammad 41–3
Angling Times 130
appearances, deceptiveness of
    144–5
Armstrong, Neil 6–7

balance
    left and right brain 27–8
    life 10–11, 45–6, 89
belief systems 64–70, 72–4,
    99–100, 154–5
blame 96
books, influence of 84, 144
brain 27–32, 37
    brain of three parts 28–31
    brainwaves 33–4
    left and right brain 27–8
    limbic system 30–1

mental rehearsal 42–3, 115–18
neo cortex 27, 30, 31
reptilian brain 29–30, 31
training 16, 17, 30–2, 74
Branson, Richard 20–4, 37
brilliance 51–3, 57, 58–9, 78, 143
brilliant Dad 54–7
Brown, David 144
Brownson, Tim 37
business 146–7, 148–9, 153–4

career 7–8, 142–3, 156
Carnegie, Dale 144
changing other people 126, 136–7
characteristics of brilliant people
    14–37
    breaking out of comfort zone
      20–6, 128–9
    competition with yourself 128
    listening to feedback 130–1
    looking beyond your sector
      129–30
    massive action 34–6
    positive action 14–20
    reframing 131–2
    stress management 32–4
    teaching 133
    thinking differently 26–32
    writing 132
checklist 158–9
choices 70, 80
Cicero 126

Circles of Influence versus Circles of Concern 75–8, 80, 154
close family 4, 80, 147, 152, 155
colleagues 5–6, 84, 136–7
comfort zone, breaking out of 20–6, 128–9
competition with yourself 128
Concern, Circle of 75fig, 76, 77, 154
confidence 25–6, 73, 77
contribution 6, 96, 132–3
control 96, 139
Covey, Stephen 75
creativity 27–8, 33, 96
criticism 130–1

Dad, brilliant 54–7
dates for achieving goals 113–14, 119–20
decisions versus actions 119–20
decluttering 156
Demosthenes 126
diaries 25–6, 119
'do it now!' 109

eating and drinking 138
Edison, Thomas 33
education 144–5, 146, 153 see also qualifications
Einstein, Albert 26
energy levels 137–8
enthusiasm 95
excitement 96
excuses, refusing to make 109
exercise 138

Facebook 90, 140
family, close 4, 80, 147, 152, 155
Farm List 85–6, 89–90
fatigue 137–8
fear 24–6, 114
feedback 130–1
Field, Peter xiv–xv

fight or flight 29–30
finances 4–5, 11, 74, 138–9, 155–6
Flatley, Michael 28
flying, September 2001 a good time for 65–8
focus 58–9, 93–4, 106–7, 148
Freebrough Community College 153
friends 5–6, 84, 136–7
fun 26, 95, 100

Gandhi, Mahatma 126, 137
garden festival 143
Gates, Bill 35–6
generosity 86, 101–2
Gestalt 41
Gitomer, Jeffrey 114
goal-setting 40–7
    90-day massive action plan xvi, 43–7, 118–20
    fear of failure 114–15
    mistakes to avoid 46
    teams 109
    three Ps technique 40–3
    timescale 113–14, 119–20
    visual representations 112–13, 114
    written goals 121
Goethe, Johann Wolfgang von 139
greed 95
groups see friends; teams
gut instinct 37

health 2–3, 11, 30, 96, 137–8
help, accepting 143
help, asking for
    how to ask 82–3
    what to ask 84–5
    who to ask 84, 85–6, 89–90
helping others 86
Hill, Napoleon 78–9
hippocampus 37
'Honest Jo(e)' 130–1

honesty
  as a value 96
  when asking for help 86
  with yourself 2, 95

'I need your help' 82–3, 86–7
ideas
  from other sectors 129–30
  sharing 132–3
images (physical) 112–13, 114
imagination (visualization)
  goals and projects 109, 114
  Mastermind Groups 79, 87–9,
    152
  mental rehearsal 42–3, 115–18
  reframing 131–2
independence 82
Influence, Circle of 75fig, 76–7, 80,
  154
influences (books and people) 84,
  136–7, 144
information overload 140
inspiration 129–30
Instagram 140
integrity see honesty
internal chatter (self-talk) 20, 72–4,
  113, 138
internet 90, 120–1, 133, 140
intuition 78–80, 88, 89
Irwin, Steve 29

Jim Carrey 112–13
Jones, Charlie 'Tremendous' 84
Jordan, Michael 128

King, Larry 35–6

language see positive language
laziness 74 see also procrastination
learning 8, 106, 139, 143–4
life lessons 142–8
Life Questions 92–5
limbic system 30–1

limiting beliefs 64, 68–70, 72–4, 75
LinkedIn 90
love 95

MacBeath, John 146
MacLean, Paul 28–9, 30
Madoff, Bernard 92
massive action 34–6, 124–6
  90-day massive action plan xvi,
    43–7, 118–20
  Rock-busting 75–80
  teams 108–9
master reframers 131–2
Mastermind Groups 78–80, 87–9,
  152
mastery of subject 106
meetings 107–8, 110, 117, 153–4
memories 37
mental rehearsal 42–3, 115–18
mentors 87 see also Mastermind
  Groups
Michael Heppell Ltd 146–8, 160–1
Michelangelo 43–4
momentum 125–6, 136
money 4–5, 11, 74, 138–9, 155–6
Mort, Paul 132
MRI scans 31
Muhammad Ali 41–3
music, motivating 109

90-day massive action plan xvi,
  43–7, 118–20
'No', saying 140
Northumberland Wildlife Trust 143

obstacles 136–40 see also
  Rock-busting techniques
Olympics 50–1, 59–61
Ornstein, Robert 27
other people
  as helpers 84, 85–6, 89–90, 143,
    146
  as obstacles 126, 136–7

talking to strangers 25
outcomes, team 106

pace 26, 107–8
passion 95
people *see* other people; relationships; teams
Percival, Allan 143
personal development 8, 139, 143–4
Personal, Positive, Present tense (three Ps) 40–3
positive action 14–20
positive goals 40–1
positive language 15–20
  the 'Brilliant' response 15–16, 36, 154
  choosing positive words 16–19
  goal-setting 40–1
  questions 19, 74
  self-talk 20, 72–4, 113, 138
  'try' is a weak word 19–20
power 95
preparation 42–3, 84–5, 115–18
present tense 41–2
presentations 118
procrastination 35–6, 74, 108–9, 136, 155–6

qualifications 77
questions
  Life Questions 92–5
  power of 19, 74

reading 84, 144
recession 148–9
recognition 96, 99–100
Red Carnation Hotels 57–8
reframing 131–2
rehearsal, mental 42–3, 115–18
rejection 96
relationships
  close family 4, 80, 147, 152, 155

creating a Farm List 85–6, 89–90
friends and colleagues 5–6, 84, 136–7
mentors 87
relaxation 32–4
reports, team 110
reprogramming your brain 16, 17, 30–2, 74
reptilian brain 29–30, 31
resources 119, 138–9 *see also* help, asking for; money; time
reward systems 109, 154
Riverdance 28
Robbins, Tony 14, 74
Rock-busting techniques
  changing self-talk 72–4
  Circles of Influence versus Circles of Concern 75–8
  Mastermind Groups 78–80, 87–9, 152
  see also obstacles
Rock, the 69–70, 72, 80, 109
rules for values 99–102

saying 'No' 140
scheduling 113–14, 119–20
schools 144–6, 153
sector, looking beyond your 129–30
security 96
self-talk 20, 72–4, 113, 138
Selye, Hans 32
September 2001 65–8
setbacks 139
sharing ideas 132–3
sleep 33–4
SMART goals 40, 47
social media 90, 121, 133, 140
society, contribution to 6, 96, 132–3
Sperry, Roger 27
sport 116–17, 118, 154–5
Stock, Rachael 147
strangers, talking to 25

stress, managing 32–4
success 78–9, 80, 82, 89, 95, 100, 106, 146–7

Take 2 32
taxi drivers 37
teaching 133, 144–5, 147, 153
teams 26, 104–10, 153–4
  ending 110
  setting up 104–6
  steps for brilliance 106–9
  West Wing 107–8
technology 120–1 *see also* social media
television 33–4
Templeton, Sir John 92
thinking differently 26–32 *see also* affirmations; belief systems
30-day challenges 15–16, 18–19
thought versus action 14–15
three Ps goal-setting 40–3
time 73
tiredness 137–8
transferable ideas 129–30, 152
true will versus false will xiv–xv
truth *see* honesty
'try' as a weak word 19–20
Twitter 140

value, adding 148–9

values 92
  being changed by 101–2
  creating new 98–101
  current 95–8
  lessons learned 147, 148–9, 155
vision 6–7, 112–21
visual representations (physical) 112–13, 114
visualization (imagination)
  goals and projects 109, 114
  Mastermind Groups 79, 87–9, 152
  mental rehearsal 42–3, 115–18
  reframing 131–2

Walker, Steve 106–7
The Waltons 4
water 138
weeds 14–15
West Wing teams 107–8, 110
Wheel of Life 2–11, 3fig, 45–6, 124, 152
willpower xiv–xv, 37
Woodroffe, Simon 139
words *see* positive language
work 7–8, 142–3, 156
work colleagues 5–6, 84, 136–7
worry 96 *see also* Concern, Circle of
writing 132, 133, 147–8

RECEIVE 90 DAYS OF *BRILLIANCE* PLUS SOME POWERFUL FREE BONUSES

If you have enjoyed *How to Be Brilliant* and you would like more resources to help you on your quest for brilliance, including:

★ a bonus chapter

★ an audio programme

★ '90 Days' – our special 12-week personal development programme

★ a regular newsletter packed with motivation, hints and tips

then take action and visit **www.michaelheppell.com** now and sign up for our free newsletter.

Tell us you've read *How to Be Brilliant* and we'll send you these extra goodies too.

Get connected

Follow Michael on Twitter @MichaelHeppell

Connect to Facebook **www.Facebook.com/MichaelHeppellOfficial**

MICHAEL HEPPELL **LIVE**

Michael Heppell has been described as one of the top three professional speakers in the world. The London Business Forum compared his style to 'like shot-gunning a bucket of espresso'. Over half a million people have seen Michael live and he consistently receives the highest marks at any event.

*If you would like to book **MICHAEL HEPPELL**
or would like information about Michael speaking at your
conference, event or to your organization, please
contact the Michael Heppell team:*

Telephone: 08456 733 336 (international: +44 1434 688 555)

Email: **info@michaelheppell.com**

Visit: **www.michaelheppell.com**

MEDIA *ENQUIRIES*

Michael is available for comment on a range of topics. He has been featured on BBC Radio 2 and Radio 4, many current affairs shows and in dozens of newspapers and magazines.

If you would like Michael to comment, write an article or be a guest on a show, please contact:

Telephone: 08456 733 336 (international: +44 1434 688 555)

Email: **info@michaelheppell.com**

Visit **www.michaelheppell.com**